Garner's Rights of Way
and
Access to the Countryside

Garner's
Rights of Way
and
Access to the Countryside

Sixth Edition

J F Garner LLD
Solicitor, Professor Emeritus
of Public Law, University of Nottingham

Edited by
A R Mowbray LLB (Hons), PhD
Lecturer in Law, University of Nottingham

With practitioners' contributions by
R G Barlow LLB (Hons), Dip LG, Solicitor of
Browne Jacobson Solicitors, Nottingham

© Longman Group UK Ltd 1993

ISBN 0752 0000 98

Published by
Longman Law, Tax and Finance
Longman Group UK Ltd
21–27 Lamb's Conduit Street
London WC1N 3NJ

Associated Offices
Australia, Hong Kong, Malaysia, Singapore, USA

First edition 1965
Second edition 1969
Third edition 1974
Fourth edition 1982
Reprinted 1984
Fifth edition 1989
Sixth edition 1993

A CIP catalogue record for this book is available
from the British Library

Printed and bound in Great Britain by Loader Jackson Printers.

Contents

Preface

For the sixth edition of this most established work I am asked by Professor Garner, again, to act as editor. The text seeks to continue his clear exposition of the law contained in earlier editions of the book. In addition, Richard Barlow of Browne Jacobson Solicitors, Nottingham, has contributed valuable insights (including three appendices of practice materials) from the perspective of an active practitioner in this field of law. I would also like to thank the publishers for their support in the preparation of this edition.

This edition encompasses major new legislation including the Access to Neighbouring Land Act 1992, the Rights of Way Act 1990 and the Planning Acts 1990. Important developments in the case law have also been incorporated in many new decisions, including the House of Lords' rulings in *Attorney General (ex rel Yorkshire Derwent Trust Ltd) v Brotherton* [1992] and the Court of Appeal's judgment in *R v Secretary of State for the Environment ex p Simms* [1990].

The law is stated as at 1 September 1993.

Alastair R Mowbray
September 1993

Biographies

Professor J F Garner is a retired solicitor and Professor Emeritus of Public Law at the University of Nottingham. As well as a scholar he is a respected practitioner in the law governing public and private rights of way. He has extensive experience, having worked with planning and highway authorities in the country, and is currently a consultant with the leading Nottingham firm, Browne Jacobson. He is also the author of *Garner's Environmental Law* (Butterworth) and *Countryside Law*, J F Garner and B L Jones (Shaw & Sons, 1993).

Dr Alastair Mowbray is an experienced Lecturer in Law at the University of Nottingham. Specialising in rights of way, he is the editor of the 5th edition of this work (1989). Dr Mowbray is also the author of *Architect's Legal Handbook* (Butterworth, 1990) and *Cases and Materials on Administrative Law* (with S H Bailey and B C Jones, Sweet and Maxwell, 1992). He has published many papers in legal and scientific journals.

Richard Barlow is a solicitor with Browne Jacobson of Nottingham. He has broad experience of acting for highway authorities, particularly Hertfordshire County Council, and of advising corporate and private clients on rights of way issues. He has contributed to the work and included a number of precedents in the new appendices, designed to assist the busy practitioner in this field.

Note

In this book reference is made to the following Acts:
The Highways Act 1959 ('the 1959 Act'), the National Parks and
Access to the Countryside Act 1949 ('the 1949 Act'), the Highways
Act 1980 ('the 1980 Act'), the Wildlife and Countryside Act 1981
('the 1981 Act'). Reference is also made to 'the definitive map'—
this is the definitive map of rights of way prepared under the 1949
Act.

Table of Cases

xiii

Table of Statutes

xxi

Table of Statutory Instruments

Chapter 1

Rights of Way—Generally

1 Introduction

The law of rights of way is part of the common law, but it has been greatly affected by statute, the most important being the Highways Act 1980 (a consolidating Act which replaced the reforming Act of 1959, itself replacing the Highway Act 1835).

A right of way is classified as a right of property, but can also be described as a right of passing over someone else's property, as the Romans called it, a *ius in re aliena*. The right carries with it no interest whatever in the soil of the land, which remains the property of the owner, although, as was said by Lord Selborne LC in *Goodson v Richardson* (1874) LR 9 Ch 221 'he cannot use the soil or deal with it by breaking it open or in any other manner so as to interfere with the use of it'. The owner of the land over which the way passes is entitled, however, to prevent its surface being used in any manner or for any purpose other than that of passing and re-passing (see p. 65).

Rights of way are either public or private. In *Hawkins v Rutter* (1892) 1 QB 668 Lord Coleridge CJ observed that the 'term "easement" has somewhat loosely and perhaps inaccurately, but still with sufficient accuracy for some purposes, been said to define a public right of way', but that in strictness it was generally only applicable to a private right, which is an 'easement', an incorporeal right in the nature of a privilege which has been created by grant or by reservation or by prescription; see also per Cozens-Hardy MR in *Woodman v Pwllbach Colliery* [1915] AC 634. In English usage, therefore, only private rights of way are thought of as being easements, a public right of way lacking the essential requirement of a dominant tenement for the benefit of which the right is exercisable. (In America, however, public rights in highways are often described

1

as easements.) The right to use a highway adheres to the public as such, although in many cases the 'top crust' may belong to the highway authority; a public right of way is thus different in kind from the rights of a public utility such as British Gas or a water company to run mains services through privately owned land, which may properly be described as an 'easement'.

There may be a private right of way and a public right of way existing along the same road at the same time, and the extinguishment of one right will not affect the other (*Walsh v Oates* (1953) 1 QB 578).

Any public right of way of any width is a highway. The Highway Act 1835, s 5 says that the term 'highways' is to be understood to mean 'all roads, bridges (not being county bridges), carriageways, cartways, horseways, bridleways, footways, causeways, churchways, and pavements'.

The great consolidating and amending Highways Act 1959 left this definition alone, but it is, of course, of importance only as a means of interpreting the unrepealed portions of the 1835 Act. The 1959 Act has been replaced by that of 1980, which in its turn does not really define the word at all, except that for the purposes of that Act, and also except where the context otherwise requires, we are told

'highway' means the whole or a part of a highway other than a ferry or waterway (s 328(1)).

Moreover, there are many roads and bridges which are not highways over which private individuals or groups of individuals have a right of passage. The older definitions make it clear that the essential characteristic of a highway is *a thoroughfare open to all subjects of the Queen to pass along on their lawful occasions*. A footpath along which every member of the public as such is entitled to pass is therefore a 'highway' just as much as a wide road may be a highway. In *Brandon v Barnes* [1966] 1 WLR 1505, an access way between market stalls linking a carriageway with a public footpath was held to be capable of being a public highway. 'Churchways' and 'occupation' roads which are restricted to the use of the inhabitants of a particular house, hamlet, village or parish, or of the tenants of a particular estate or manor, are not highways, though in process of time they may change into public ways (see *Brocklebank v Thompson* [1903] 2 Ch 344 dealing generally with 'customary' ways, and see p 109 et seq; as to 'churchways', see p 18).

There have been, moreover, two types of highways since the

passing of the Highway Act 1835, namely, those which are repairable by the inhabitants at large, and those which are not so repairable—under the Highways Act 1980 these are now known as highways maintainable at the public expense, and highways not so maintainable (see p 50). A 'private street', which is not maintainable at the public expense, may nonetheless be (but need not be) a highway over which the public have acquired rights to pass and repass. 'Road' is not a term of art in highway law, although any road in fact open to the public (whether or not as *of right*) may be a road for the purposes of the Road Traffic Acts provided there is sufficient public use of it (*Kreft v Rawcliffe* (1984) *The Times*, 12 May).

The concept of a highway is as old as the common law itself, but statutes have made many changes. The law was first consolidated in the Highways Act 1959, but this was amended in 1961 and 1971, and the principal Act is now the Highways Act 1980, which repeals almost all the earlier legislation. Since then the Wildlife and Countryside Act 1981 has made further amendments to that branch of highway law with which we are concerned.

2 Places of recreation not highways

It has been held that a racecourse is not necessarily a highway (*Earl of Coventry v Willes* (1863) 28 JP 453); nor are parks or commons and open spaces, such as village greens, which local residents have the right to use for recreation or otherwise; and, although many such places are used by the general public from time to time without interference, that does not convert them into highways, as a highway is a right to pass from one point to another along a defined route (see p 65). However, the Court of Appeal has recently held that a circular pathway around a lake could be a right of way (*Dyfed County Council v Secretary of State for Wales* (1990) 59 P & CR 275). A cul-de-sac may be a highway, especially if it leads to some definite place, such as a church, or some object such as an ancient monument (*Tyne Improvement Commissioners v Imrie* (1899) 81 LT 174; *Eyre v New Forest Highway Board* (1892) 56 JP 517). A cul-de-sac will not, however, be presumed to be a highway by virtue of mere user without evidence of expenditure on it by the public authority (*Att-Gen v Antrobus* [1905] 2 Ch 188), where it was held that no right can be granted (otherwise than by statute: see p 102) to the public at large to wander at will over an undefined open space. This is not to say, however, that a cul-de-sac can never be a highway, as such a way may be dedicated to public use as may any other, but the facts may be more difficult to establish in the case of a cul-de-sac; eg the *Stonehenge* case (*Att-Gen v Antrobus*) was expressly approved in *Re Ellenborough Park* [1956] Ch 131 at p 153, although it was there held that such a right could be created by deed as an easement in favour of private individuals or owners of specific dominant tenements. Presumably such a private easement could also be acquired by prescription.

A curious idea prevalent in some quarters that the 'passage of a corpse' establishes a public right of way was disposed of by *Belton v Nicholas* (1935) 79 SJ 25.

3 Purposes for which a right of way may be enjoyed

A highway may be enjoyed by members of the public only to pass and re-pass on their lawful occasions; they may not (for example) use the right to interfere with the lawful activities of a neighbouring landowner (*Harrison v Duke of Rutland* (1893) 1 QB 142), nor to park a car while trespassing in a neighbouring field (*Randall v Tarrant* [1955] 1 WLR 255). Nor may they pick wild flowers protected under Pt I of the 1981 Act. The Court of Appeal has expressed the view that the use of paths for recreational walking is capable of giving rise to the possibility of deemed dedication as a right of way (*Dyfed County Council v Secretary of State for Wales* (1990) 59 P & CR 275).

4 'General' and 'limited' rights

A distinction has been drawn between 'general' and 'limited' rights of passage, which is not altogether satisfactory, because there can be no 'general' user in a private right of way, the grant being for some limited purposes of the owner of the dominant tenement and being specified when the easement is granted. These limited purposes may be of various kinds (see p 110). In contrast, the public may enjoy highways generally, for all purposes of passing and repassing at all times and seasons without distinction of traffic, or the public right may be to use the way on foot only or with animals, or with vehicles. Under the Highways Act 1980 the Secretary of

State for Transport may exclude certain specified classes of traffic (eg pedestrians or animals: see Sched 4) from using 'special' roads (ie principally, motorways).

5 Carriageways, bridleways and footways

A carriageway, ie a way of passage for carts and carriages, is the form of highway giving the largest kind of public rights. It covers rights of footway, bridleway and driftway unless the two latter are specifically excluded (see *Ballard v Dyson* (1808) 1 Taunt 279).

At common law a driftway ('drive way', sometimes termed 'park way') is the term applied to a way for driving cattle or riding horses, and it includes the right of footway and bridleway. However, the driftway is no longer of any significance in modern law. (Although it is unknown to statute law, a right of driftway could presumably still be established at common law. However, it could not be shown as such on the definitive map.) A right of bridleway (ie for the passage of horses and now, bicycles: Countryside Act 1968, s 30) does not necessarily include also a right of driftway, though it does include a footway (see definition of 'bridleway' in s 66(1) of the 1981 Act). A right of bridleway does not include a right of passage for vehicles of any sort other than bicycles, and a cyclist must give way to pedestrians and persons on horseback. A footpath *simpliciter* gives a right of passage for pedestrians only with or without normal size perambulators (see p 24). These common law meanings of 'footpath' and 'bridleway' are adapted slightly for the purposes of the current legislation. However, in these statutes, a bridleway may include a drift or drive way, and a 'footpath' does not include a public way at the side of a public road. 'Footway', on the other hand, is defined in the 1980 Act, s 329(1) as meaning 'a way comprised in a highway which also comprises a carriageway, being a way over which the public have a right of way on foot only'. 'Public path' is the compendious term used in the Acts to include both a public footpath and a public bridleway.

In the definitive maps prepared under the 1949 Act, some bridleways were described as 'roads used as public paths'; under the Countryside Act 1968 and the 1981 Act, s 54 however, these were required to be reclassified either as 'byways open to all traffic', 'bridleways', or 'footpaths' (see p 30).

6 Walkways

A different form of public footpath may be created by agreement between the owner of an existing or future building and the local highway authority, under the Highways Act 1980, s 35. Such an agreement may provide for a way through the building to be made available as a public right of way, subject to limitations and conditions and rights reserved to the building owner. The agreement will normally make provision for the maintenance, cleansing, drainage and lighting of the walkway, and the highway authority may make byelaws regulating, *inter alia*, the conduct of persons using the walkways.

7 Wheeled traffic

The right of carriageway may be taken to cover the right of passage for all wheeled traffic, subject to any express exclusion on dedication, and subject also to the provisions of modern legislation excluding particular traffic and providing for cases of use by traffic likely to cause damage and imposing a liability to repair.

Bicycles and tricycles are 'carriages' within the meaning of the Highways Acts (Local Government Act 1888, s 85), and therefore it is an offence under the Highway Act 1835, s 72 (left unrepealed by the 1959 and 1980 Acts) to ride such a carriage on a 'footpath', which means in this context a footpath or causeway at the side of a road: *R v Pratt* (1867) LR 3 QB 64. Similarly, it seems that a bicycle may not be ridden where a right of footway only can be shown, but a pedal cycle ('not being a motor vehicle') may be ridden on a bridleway, provided the cyclist gives way to pedestrians and persons on horseback (Countryside Act 1968, s 30). This right may be restricted by byelaws (made, eg under the Local Government Act 1972, s 235) or an order of a local authority. Cycle racing is prohibited on a public road or bridleway, but may be allowed by departmental authorisation given under regulations (Road Traffic Act 1972, s 20). On the other hand, the county or London borough council may authorise a motor vehicle trial to be held on a footpath or bridleway, under the Road Traffic Act 1972, s 35 as amended by the Local Government Act 1972, Sched 19, provided that written consent has been given by the owner and occupier of the land over which the way runs. Motor vehicles may not be driven on any common or other land not forming part of a road, or on a footpath (an expression which here apparently includes a footway: see s 196(1) of the 1972 Act) or bridleway (Road Traffic Act 1972, s 36).

In *R v Mathias* (1861) 2 F & F 570, it was held that the use of a footway may include the use of a perambulator as being a usual accompaniment of a pedestrian, provided it is of such a size and weight as not to cause inconvenience to other pedestrians and not to injure the soil. Whether, in the circumstances, the use of such a vehicle is justifiable or not is a question of fact; see generally as to obstructive nuisances on highways, *R v Bartholomew* [1908] 1 KB 554, and see p 91.

A road traffic order (restricting the use of the way by specified classes of traffic) may be made in respect of a footpath, bridleway or by-way open to all traffic, under the Road Traffic Regulation Act 1984. An order could thus be made prohibiting the driving of motor cycles or riding horses on a by-way otherwise open to all traffic where the highway authority (generally the county council) considers such a restriction expedient so as to, *inter alia*, avoid danger to other users, preserve the character of a right of way which is especially suitable for pedestrians; and to improve the amenity of the surrounding area (Road Traffic Regulation Act 1984, s 1, as amended by the New Roads and Street Works Act 1991). In addition the Secretary of State may make a similar order for rights of way in the National Parks and other areas of outstanding natural beauty for the purpose of promoting public enjoyment of these areas (1984 Act, s 22).

8 Seashore rights

Contrary to popular belief, there is no public right of way along or across the foreshore unless such a right has been dedicated (see *Blundell v Catterall* (1821) 5 B & Ald 268); but see, as to this, the effect of the findings of the Court of Appeal in *Williams-Ellis v Cobb* (p 21). On the other hand, the inhabitants of a parish or village may have acquired rights for themselves which the public generally are allowed to enjoy without hindrance. Thus, in *Mercer v Denne* [1904] 2 Ch 534 a custom was proved for local fishermen to dry their nets; in *Ramsgate Corporation v Debling* (1906) 22 TLR 369, the court held that a claim by the inhabitants to place chairs on the seashore was not proved, and that such a right could not be claimed under the Prescription Act 1832; and see also *Llandudno Urban District Council v Woods* [1899] 2 Ch 705. In *Beckett Ltd v Lyons*

[1967] Ch 449, a claim was made for the inhabitants of the County
Palatine of Durham to remove sea-coal from a particular foreshore
in the county. The claim was denied by the Court of Appeal for
lack of sufficient evidence, and as Harman and Winn LJJ said, the
right was not of a nature that could be acquired by a fluctuating
body of persons such as the inhabitants of a county.

9 Highways by water

The relationship between rights of way over land and public rights
of navigation has recently been considered by the House of Lords
in *Att-Gen (ex rel Yorkshire Derwent Trust Ltd) v Brotherton* [1992] 1
All ER 230. The case concerned the plaintiffs' desire to assert a
public right of navigation on non-tidal reaches of the river Derwent
in Yorkshire which was disputed by the defendants, who were
riparian owners of the land adjoining the river. Lord Oliver stated:

Now there are, of course, obvious analogies which can be drawn between
traffic on land and waterborne traffic. Both involve the passage of men or
vehicles above or on the surface of the ground in a given direction—a
characteristic which they also share with air traffic. It would be surprising,
therefore, if at least some of the incidents of a right of passage by water
were not compared analogically with those of a right of passage by land.
For instance, since both involve passage across or through private property
one would expect to find as indeed one does find, that the origins of both
lie in grant or presumed grant by the owner of the soil over or through
which they pass. But, as has been mentioned in several of the cases cited,
the analogy is not a perfect one (see, for instance, *Simpson v AG* [1904] AC
476 at 509 per Lord Lindley) and there are obvious differences between a
highway on land and a waterway.

Thus a public right on land depends upon proof of public user over an
exactly demonstrated course, whereas a river exists permanently and as a
natural feature; . . . Equally, a right of navigation may, it seems, according
to the nature of the locus, embrace the right to navigate in no defined
channel over the whole surface of an inland lake (see *Marshall v Ulleswater
Steam Navigation Co Ltd* (1871) LR 7 QB 166 at 172). Further, there is,
apart from statute or custom, no person under the obligation of keeping
the banks in repair or the channel free for navigation; and if the stream
dries up or becomes choked there is no right either to deviate or to trespass
upon the soil in order to clear it. Moreover, it may embrace simply the
passage of articles without human accompaniment (for instance, the floating
of logs on the current either singly or in rafts) and involves ordinary
incidents peculiar to the medium of its exercise and inapplicable to land
transport, such as the right to moor or to drop anchor on the soil of the

river bed for purposes incidental to passage (see *AG (ex rel Moore) v Wright* (1897) 2 QB 318 at 321) (at p 245).

The House went on to consider whether a public right of navigation could be a right of way 'over any land' for the purposes of s 1(1) of the Rights of Way Act 1932 (*see below* p 36). Having ascertained the background to the Act:

The mischief which the Act was intended to cure was the difficulty which had arisen in relation to public footpaths and ways and there is no suggestion that any problem had arisen in relation to waterways or that waterways were in anybody's contemplation as giving rise to any problem at the date of the Act (*per* Lord Oliver at p 248).

His Lordship then examined the ordinary meaning of the phrase and observed:

One can properly describe a cart track, for instance, as a 'way across the field' but nobody, even a lawyer, would ordinarily apply that description to a river. I cannot, for instance, think that any reader of Alfred Lord Tennyson would have regarded the Lady of Shalott, as she floated down to Camelot through the noises of the night, as exercising a right of way over the subjacent soil (at p 246).

Therefore, his Lordship concluded (with the unanimous agreement of his brethren) that s 1(1) applies to 'a physical path or track situate on the land itself' and not to public rights of navigation over inland waters.

A commentator has concluded that the *Yorkshire Derwent Trust* decision, 'in excluding waterways from the ambit of s 1 of the Rights of Way Act 1932 the House of Lords has clarified the law but confirmed the difficulties of establishing the existence of public rights of navigation on non-tidal rivers' (D Wilkinson, [1992] JPL 526). Generally, public rights of navigation can only be created:

(1) by express or implied dedication by the riparian owner of the river bed;

(2) by user from time immemorial (1189) (eg right of navigation on the river Trent recognised in *Mayor of Nottingham v Lambert* (1738) Willes 111); and

(3) by an Act of Parliament.

Inland waterways vested in the British Waterways Board are now divided into commercial waterways, cruising waterways and others, and whereas the public are not expressly given any rights to use waterways of the Board, there is a general duty imposed on the Board to maintain commercial and cruising waterways, 'with a view to securing the general availability of [such] waterways for public use' (Transport Act 1968, ss 104, 105). An access agreement or order may be made in respect of other waterways belonging to the Board (*ibid*, s 111, and see p 103).

For the popular Norfolk and Suffolk Broads a new statutory body (the Broads Authority) has been created to, *inter alia*, protect the interests of navigation and promote the enjoyment of the area by the public: Norfolk and Suffolk Broads Act 1988, ss 1 and 2. The authority must appoint a specialist navigation committee and consult with the committee on the making of byelaws to develop good management of the designated navigation area, whilst conserving the natural beauty and amenities of the area (1988 Act, ss 9 and 10).

10 Towpaths

The legal position regarding the rights of the public on towpaths (running alongside a navigable river or a canal) has been dealt with in several cases.

In *Grand Junction Canal Co v Petty* (1888) 21 QBD 273, the appellants were owners of land which they had acquired for the purposes of a towpath, and they took proceedings against the respondents for trespass. The defence was that it was a public footpath and the jury found that there was no trespass. The appellants then sought to set aside the verdict on the ground that their special statute gave them no power to dedicate a towpath to the public, but the Court of Appeal held that there was nothing in the statute inconsistent with their granting a right of way (*see R v Inhabitants of Leake* (1833) S B & Ad 469) and Lord Esher MR in his judgment said that such a dedication was not to be taken to be absolute and without limitation.

It must be, I think, a dedication to the public of the towing-path for the purpose of such user as a footpath as will not interfere with its ordinary use as a towing-path by the company. I do not think that the people walking on the towing-path are entitled to say that the towing must be regulated with reference to their convenience. The public in accepting the dedication must be taken to accept it as a limited dedication and cannot set up a right to prevent or limit the user of the towing-path by the company. If the horse or the towrope and the foot-passenger are in one another's way, the foot-passenger must look out for himself and get out of the way.

In *Thames Conservators v Kent* [1918] 2 KB 272, the Court of Appeal dealt with the position of the Thames Conservators in relation to the public and adjoining landowners. The conservators by their special Act had duties as to navigation and keeping the towpaths in repair (whether or not they owned the soil) and were given power to make byelaws for preventing disorderly conduct to the annoyance of persons using the towpaths. But the Court held that the Act gave them no power to dedicate any part of the towpath as a public highway except such parts as they might actually own in fee simple, and not even those parts if such dedication was inconsistent with the proper performance of their statutory duties; nor could they prevent the public from using the towpath as a highway where it had been dedicated as such for foot-passengers and for towing purposes with horses and other draught animals.

It is now clear that a towpath is nonetheless a public right of way if it measures up to the normal tests for such a right (1981 Act, s 66(2)). Nevertheless, the Court of Appeal has recently distinguished between a public right of way by foot over a path and a public right of towage. In *Sussex Investments Ltd v Jackson* (1993) *The Times*, 29 July, Balcombe LJ stated that the latter right included the right to pass a towrope from the horse or other beast of burden on the towpath to the vessel being towed and might include a right to pass and re-pass from the vessel being towed to the land. But, neither a public right of way nor a public right of towage entitled houseboat owners to attach moorings or gangplanks to the banks of a river which were in private ownership.

11 Bridges

Bridges are of two kinds: those which continue highways over actual watercourses, and those which may more properly be termed viaducts, not being over watercourses. Over such structures there may exist a public right of way just as over any other highway; and at common law the inhabitants at large may be liable for maintenance. But from the earliest times the county and not the parish has been the authority, so far as bridges are concerned, representing the 'inhabitants at large', and liability extended to 300 ft from each side of a bridge under the charge of a highway authority (Statute of Bridges 1530–31 22 Hen 8 c 5).

Many bridges have been erected over streams and depressions by private persons for their own convenience, eg where a right of way had been created before 1960, where a public roadway crossed a stream and the owner put up a bridge and allowed the public to use it, that bridge became part of the public highway. If the bridge falls down, the public must cross as before by wading through the stream until the highway authority repairs it. The landowner could not be compelled to do so unless he or his predecessors in title for some special reason have placed themselves under an obligation not only to erect such a bridge but to maintain it (for instance, under the terms of an inclosure award). Not every structure of this sort is legally a 'bridge'—erections over roadside ditches, and drain culverts, may or may not come under that description.

However, no new bridge could become part of the highway after 1960, by virtue of the Highways Act 1959, s 23. Railway bridges provided for in the Railways Clauses Consolidation Act 1845, ss 46, 49 and 52 are normally the responsibility of the British Railways Board under the Transport Act 1962. (As to the repair of bridges, see p 63.)

12 Discovering the existence of a public right of way

A person may seek to discover the existence of a public right of way across or near land they own or propose to purchase by the following investigations. First, where a prospective purchaser is considering buying a property, his professional adviser can make specific enquiries of the local authority in whose area the property is located. These enquiries are in addition to the ordinary local land charges search and relevant questions are found on the standard forms Con 29A (for district councils) and Con 29D (for the London borough councils). The selection of appropriate questions will enable the purchaser to discover, *inter alia*, if rights of way crossing the property are maintainable at public expense and whether there are any proposals to construct new rights of way within 200 metres of the property. Secondly, an individual may personally inspect the list of highways currently maintainable at public expense, which is available at both district and county council offices by virtue of the Highways Act 1980, s 36(6). The obvious limitation of this record is that highways not maintainable by the public are excluded from the list (see further, p 50). Finally, an examination of the definitive map (copies of which must be made available in each district and so far as practicable in each parish covered by the map). The 1981 Act, s 57(5)) prepared by the appropriate survey authority (generally county councils) under the Wildlife and Countryside Act 1981, will show the various categories of public rights of way recorded by the authority. These maps are conclusive evidence of the existence of a public right of way of at least the form recorded (eg a footpath or a bridleway). However, the enquirer must bear in mind the fact that these maps are subject to review and can be modified to include a previously unrecorded right of way (see p 25).

Chapter 2

The Express Creation and Extent of Public Rights of Way

1 The creation of public rights of way

Public rights of way arise in two ways: they are either provided for by legislation, or they are created by dedication of the soil to public use by the owner and acceptance by the public. It is sometimes claimed that the right may arise by prescription, but the principles of the common law of prescription and the Prescription Act 1832 only apply to private as opposed to public rights, and it is desirable, in order to avoid difficulty in a case where long user may be the basis of a claim, to prove facts which would justify the presumption of dedication.

Where there has been evidence of a user by the public so long and in such a manner that the owner of the fee, whoever he was, must have been aware that the public were acting under the belief that the way had been dedicated and has taken no steps to disabuse them of that belief, it is not conclusive evidence, but evidence on which those who have to find the fact *may* find that there was a dedication by the owner, whoever he was. It is therefore, in England, never practically necessary to rely on prescription to establish a public way (*per* Lord Blackburn in *Mann v Brodie* (1885) 10 App Cas 378).

Further explanation of Lord Blackburn's dictum may be found in the judgment of Buckley J in *Att-Gen v Esher Linoleum Co Ltd* [1901] 2 Ch 647:

In all these cases of right of way it is necessary to remember that the thing to be established is dedication, not user. A highway is not acquired by user. You cannot acquire a right of public way under the Prescription Acts. If you want to acquire a right by prescription you must go back to the time of Richard I — to a time before legal memory. In most of these cases dedication, it is true, is proved by user. But user is the evidence to prove dedication; it is not user, but dedication, which constitutes the highway.

14

Again, while public user may be evidence of dedication, it will be good for that purpose only when it is exercised under such conditions as to imply the assertion of a right with the knowledge and acquiescence of the owner of the fee (per Lord Kinnear in *Folkestone Corporation v Brockman* [1914] AC 338. But under the Highways Act 1980, s 31 (replacing the Rights of Way Act 1932 and the 1959 Act, s 34), if user is proved for the period of 20 years there is a *præsumptio juris* of dedication subject to the conditions in s 31 being fulfilled (per Scott LJ in *Jones v Bates* [1938] 2 All ER 237 at p 246). As to the relevance of the Prescription Act provisions in interpreting s 31 see the judgment of Hilbery J in *Merstham Manor Ltd v Coulsdon and Purley Urban District Council*, (see p 37); and, as will appear later (see pp 16 and 83), dedication itself implies an intention to dedicate: see *Barraclough v Johnson* (1838) 7 LJQB 172; *Att-Gen (ex parte Weymouth Corporation) v Bird* (1936) *The Times*, 9 July.

In the case of a bridleway or footpath, proof of dedication and acceptance will still be sufficient to establish a public right of way, even if it is not recorded on the definitive map (see p 25).

2 Creation by statute

The extent to which highways can be created by statute can be found in the numerous Inclosure Acts empowering commissioners to enclose lands subject to the construction of roads for the benefit of the public. Some of these statutes give authority for the making of roads without providing for that authority to be exercised. In several cases trouble has arisen by reason of the fact that the statutory powers had never been exercised and there had been no user by the public and therefore no acceptance (*Cubitt v Maxse* (1873) LR 8 CP 704). Where, however, there is an unfinished highway which the public have regularly used, adoption will be presumed (see eg *R v Lordsmere* (1850) 15 QB 689, where the inhabitants were held liable for repair in consequence). In *Sheringham Urban District Council v Holsey* (1904) 68 JP 395, a public footpath created under an Inclosure Act had been used for wheeled traffic; the court held that this was illegal — there having been no dedication for that purpose.

Any existing roadway may be converted into a highway by Act of Parliament. Moreover, any person or body of persons may be authorised by statute to make a highway or highways. Under the

Development and Road Improvement Funds Act 1909, power was given to the Road Board to construct new highways and for that purpose to acquire the necessary land, and a similar power is now vested in the Secretary of State for Transport and in the local highway authority by the Highways Act 1980, s 24 (as affected by the Transfer of Functions (Transport) Order 1981 (SI No 238)). Every such highway is maintainable at the public expense, by virtue of s 36 of the 1980 Act. Again, new highways may be created under the Housing Act 1985, s 13, and other statutes such as the New Towns Act 1981, s 11.

A new private street may be declared to be a highway where land has been defined in the development plan and designated for the purposes of s 232 of the 1980 Act. New roads may be constructed under the trunk road and special road powers vested in the Secretary of State under the Highways Act 1980, Pt II. Under the Highways Act 1980, Pt III the following powers exist for the creation of new public rights of way ('public paths'):

(a) by creation agreement between the council of a county, London borough or district, or the Common Council of the City of London, or a joint planning board in a National Park, and the person having the necessary power to dedicate the land (s 25 of the 1980 Act);

or

(b) by the making of a compulsory 'public path creation order' by such a local authority or board, in accordance with the procedure laid down in the 1980 Act (s 26) and the Public Path Orders Regulations 1993 (SI No 11).

In either case the local authority or board (or in some cases the highway authority) must survey the path and carry out any work considered necessary to make up the site of the path (s 27 of the 1980 Act).

In addition, the Countryside Commission (Countryside Council for Wales, in the Principality) may take action for the establishment of a 'long-distance route' under the 1949 Act, ss 51–55 (as amended by the Environmental Protection Act 1990, Sched 11). These provisions do not give new powers for the creation of rights of way, but powers are given for the provision of accommodation and ferries, etc, along the course of such routes. They have been used to bring into existence as public rights of way, *inter alia*, the Pennine Way, the Cleveland Way in Yorkshire, and the coastguard cliff path in Cornwall.

Highways created under statutory powers do not require any

public acceptance; provided the conditions of the statute under which they have been created are complied with, they are highways as soon as they have been opened for public use.

3 Dedication and acceptance

Apart from ways created by statute, no right of way can be created except by dedication and acceptance—the latter simply meaning user by the public. Such user need not necessarily be immediate. Some length of time may elapse before the public actually begin to make use of the way and thus secure the public right, but delay extending over a long period may be a matter of importance should any question of dedication and acceptance arise at some period later. There are, moreover, several other important factors to be taken into account such as:

(1) the distinction between dedication and mere *licence*;
(2) the right or capacity to dedicate;
(3) the extent of the dedication; and
(4) what, if any, special reservations were made by the dedicator.

These require to be considered separately as questions of fact when any question of dedication arises. For cases on dedication and acceptance, see *Cubitt v Maxse* (1873) LR 8 CP 704 (both dedication and acceptance necessary, but public not obliged to accept the use of a way when offered to them); *Healey v Batley Corporation* (1874) LR 19 Eq 375 (scheme abandoned); *Att-Gen v Biphosphated Guano Co* (1879) 11 ChD 327 (agreement to dedicate insufficient).

4 Dedication—express or implied

Dedication may be either express or implied. Express dedication can be shown only when the actual facts and circumstances under which a landowner granted a right of way over his land to be used by the public at large can be disclosed. Generally, where the facts are known (or where a public right of way has been established under s 31 of the 1980 Act (see p 34)), no question is likely to arise. It is only when there is a difference of opinion as to whether a right of way exists that evidence becomes necessary from which it may be presumed that there was an intention on the part of the owner to dedicate this right to the public.

It is necessary to show, in order that there may be a right of way established, that it has been used openly as of right, and for so long a time that it must have come to the knowledge of the owners of the fee that the public were so using it as of right, and from this apparent acquiescence of the owners a jury might fairly draw the inference that they chose to consent in which case there would be a dedication (*per* Blackburn J in *Greenwich Board of Works v Maudslay* (1870) LR 5 QB 397, at p 404; and see p 34).

As to proof of dedication and rebutting evidence, see p 93.

5 Dedication or licence

Sometimes a landowner out of mere courtesy may allow the public to cross his land without intending thereby to grant a right of way in the legal sense (note: *Samuels* [1986] JPL 666). There is always an element of risk in so doing, but the landowner can protect himself by placing a notice 'in such manner as to be visible to persons using the way' (Act of 1980, s 31(3)(*a*), and see p 42), or by stopping the way for a short period (eg by locking the gates once a year on Good Friday or Boxing Day etc), so as to assert his rights. See *Poole v Huskinson* (1843) 11 M & W 827, confirmed by *Chinnock v Hartley Wintney RDC* (1899) 63 JP 327, with reference to the questions which arise where landowners have allowed public user without any intention of granting public rights of way, and also *Barraclough v Johnson* (1838) 7 LJ QB 172, where there was a definite agreement to pay five shillings per annum, which the court held amounted to a licence and negatived dedication.

6 Churchways

A typical 'churchway' case arose in *Att-Gen v Mallock* (1931) 146 LT 344. The plaintiffs claimed a declaration that a pathway over the defendant's land leading to Cockington Church (near Torquay) was a highway, on the ground that dedication should be presumed upon evidence of uninterrupted user by the public throughout living memory and from evidence of reputation. The church was surrounded by the defendant's grounds and, apart from a private path from his grounds, there was no access to the church except by the way in question. The defendant admitted that there was a churchway for parishioners along the way, but he denied that there was any public right of way. Since 1774 the title to the property had been such that the owners could, if so minded, have dedicated the way to the public. The freehold of the church was in the incumbent and it had fulfilled all the functions of a parish church, but no person had a right to enter it without the permission of the vicar and churchwardens when it was not open for divine service. The court found that, apart from parishioners, comparatively few persons had visited the church until about 1890, but that after the First World War large numbers of persons had used the way and no one had ever been turned back. Owing to the increased use of the way, notices were put up that visitors must keep to the path and not pick flowers, and that there would be no admission through the gate after 6 pm. There was also a notice: 'No thoroughfare except to the Church'. In 1923, annoyance from visitors began and the gate was ordered to be locked after dusk, but no complaint was ever made, though some persons were actually prevented from going along the way to the church.

The court held, upon this evidence, that the use of the way could properly be explained as having taken place by permission, and there was no reason to presume dedication. (The land in question now belongs to the local authority and the public are freely admitted by leave of the authority.) Nonetheless, it seems that in a case of this kind, the parishioners may be able to claim a way of necessity for the purpose of attending divine service only (*Shury v Piggot* (1626) 3 Bulstr 339).

Note that ecclesiastical courts do not have jurisdiction to make rulings regarding the scope of rights of way of an essentially secular nature; such rulings can only be made where they are necessarily ancillary to an application for a faculty of a kind which the court may grant: *Re St Martin le Grand, York* [1989] 2 All ER 711.

7 Capacity to dedicate

Where there has been an express dedication the only question that can arise is whether the individual or body purporting to dedicate was or is owner in fee simple, since the right of way given to the public is a right in perpetuity, and unless the dedicator is absolute owner of the land over which the right of way is to be given and there are no prior interests the dedication is valueless. Trustees and corporations whose titles are clear may dedicate provided such dedication is not incompatible with the purpose for which they exist, eg where a canal company granted a right of way over an embankment which would have led ultimately to its destruction (*Great Western Railway Co v Solihull Rural District Council* (1902) 66 JP 772; *Lancs and Yorks Railway Co v Davenport* (1906) 70 JP 129). In *British Transport Commission v Westmorland County Council* [1958] AC 126, the House of Lords approved *R v Inhabitants of Leake* (1833) 5 B & Ad 469, in which Parke B said (at p 478):

If the land were vested by the Act of Parliament in commissioners, so that they were thereby bound to use it for some special purpose, incompatible with its public use as a highway, I should have thought that such trustees would have been incapable in point of law, to make a dedication of it, but if such use by the public be not incompatible with the objects prescribed by the Act, then I think it clear that the commissioners have that power.

Since the passing of the National Parks and Access to the Countryside Act 1949, s 58 (now incorporated in the Highways Act 1980, s 31), it has been no answer to a claim of a right of way established under s 31 (p 34) or its predecessors to be able to prove that at the relevant time there was no person in possession who was capable of dedicating the way.

8 Leaseholders and tenants for life

A leaseholder has no power to dedicate a public right of way (see *Wood v Veal* (1822) 5 B & Ald 454; *R v East Mark (Inhabitants)* (1848) 11 QB 877; *Corsellis v London County Council* [1908] 1 Ch 13; and *Shearburn v Chertsey Rural District Council* (1914) 78 JP 289), and however long the public may have used a way during the occupation of tenants, that does not bind the owner unless he knew of it and acquiesced (*Thornhill v Weeks (No 3)* [1915] 1 Ch 106); and this is preserved by the closing words of s 31(1) of the 1980 Act (see p 34). The position of a tenant for life is defined by the Settled Land Act 1925, ss 50 and 56. Section 50 of that Act provides that

'a sale, exchange, lease or other authorised disposition, may be made either of land . . . or of any mines and minerals, . . . with or without a grant or reservation of . . . wayleaves or rights of way. . . .'

Section 56, *ibid*, provides that the tenant for life 'on or after or in connexion with a sale or grant for building purposes, or a building lease, or the development as a building estate of the settled land, or any part thereof, . . . for the general benefit of the residents may, *inter alia*:

(a) enter into any agreement for the recompense to be made for any part of the settled land which is required for the widening of a highway under the Highways Act 1980 (s 72), or otherwise (and he may presumably sell land for the purpose, which the authority have power to acquire by s 239, ibid); and

(b) consent to the diversion of any highway over the settled land under (s 116 of) the 1980 Act, or otherwise.

Any agreement or consent so made or given will be as valid and effectual for all purposes as if made or given by an absolute owner of the settled land: 1925 Act, s 56(2), and *Farquhar v Newbury Rural District Council* [1909] 1 Ch 12.

The presumption of dedication where property had been in strict settlement with a break is illustrated in *Williams-Ellis v Cobb* [1935] 1 KB 310. Where the owner of an estate, across which two cliff paths led to the sea at high-water mark, sought to restrain public user, evidence of public user was given by different classes of persons over the whole period of living memory. From 1856 to 1908 the property was in strict settlement, but it was admitted that there had been a period between 1820 and 1856 during which there was an owner capable of dedicating. The county court judge before whom the action was first tried held that since there was no owner capable of dedicating during the period of proved public user he could not infer dedication from such user. He also held that the ways had no sufficient *terminus ad quem*. But the Court of Appeal, applying the ruling in *Moser v Ambleside Urban District Council* (1925) 89 JP 118, held that, although the public have only limited rights over the foreshore (*Blundell v Catterall* (see p 7)), the sea may be a sufficient *terminus ad quem*, and they also held that in such a case the tribunal of fact may infer a dedication by an owner capable of dedicating at some prior date to the earliest proved user. See also *Poole v Huskinson* (1843) 11 M & W 827—dictum of Parke B at p 830; *Folkestone Corporation v Brockman* [1914] AC 338; and *Stoney v Eastbourne Rural District Council* [1927] 1 Ch 367.

9 Extent of dedication and reservations by dedicator

Although it is not competent for a landowner to dedicate a public right of way to a limited section of the public, or for a limited period of time (*Dawes v Hawkins* (1860) 8 CB (NS) 848), he may impose restrictions upon his grant. The basic principle underlying all grants of rights of way is that the owner of the land permits the public to pass over the surface of his land, by foot or by vehicle or otherwise and the public must observe and abide by the extent of the grant. Any restrictions imposed by the landowner when dedicating must be observed and the public in availing themselves of the right which has been granted must do so subject to the restrictions, whatever they may be. The public must take the way as they find it, complete with any obstructions such as trees, etc. In *Fisher v Prowse* (1862) 31 LJ QB 212, Blackburn J said:

> It is, of course, not obligatory on the owner of land to dedicate the use of it as a highway to the public. It is equally clear that it is not compulsory on the public to accept the use of way when offered to them. If the use of the soil as a way is offered by the owner to the public under given conditions and subject to certain reservations, and the public accept the use under such circumstances, there can be no injustice in holding them to the terms on which the benefit was conferred. On the other hand, great injustice and hardship would often arise if, when a public right of way has been acquired under a given state of circumstances, the owner of the soil should be held bound to alter the state of circumstances to his own disadvantage and loss, and to make further concessions to the public altogether beyond the scope of his original intention. More especially would this be the case when public rights of way have been acquired by mere user. For instance, the owner of the bank of a canal . . . may, without considering the effect of what he is doing, permit the passengers to pass along until the public have acquired a right of way there. It is often hard upon him that the public right should have been thus acquired; it would be doubly so if the consequences were that he was bound to fill up or fence off his canal.

The reference to public rights of way being acquired 'by mere user' does not fully accord with later decisions requiring *intention* to be taken into account as the ultimate basis upon which dedication may be presumed (*Barraclough v Johnson* (1838) 7 LJ QB 172, and see pp 14 and 95).

The public are entitled to use the way only as it has been dedicated, and if it has been dedicated subject to a right to plough up, for example, the public cannot complain. There is no right to deviate if the way becomes founderous unless it can be proved that there had been minimal user of such a right (*Duncomb's Case* (1634) Cro Car 366, and see *Arnold v Holbrook* (1893) LR 8 QB 96), or, presumably, such a right can be shown to have been exercised over a period of 20 years (Highways Act 1980, s 31; see p 34).

While the public must be content with what is granted, the

restrictions imposed by the owner of the land must not be such as to render the grant useless or more burdensome; for example, if a swing gate exists on a footway dedicated to the public, the owner of the soil must not subsequently remove this and cause inconvenience to the public by fixing a locked gate over which persons using the footway must climb. On the other hand, if the right of way dedicated to the public involves passing along a part that is generally, or at night time or under any special circumstances, dangerous, the public, in accepting and using the right, must take it with all risks, and the owner of the soil will not be answerable for any mishaps. (As to liability for injury arising from non-repair of public roadways, see p 53 *et seq*.)

10 Adoption of carriage roads, etc

By the Highways Act 1980, s 38(3) (as amended by the New Roads and Street Works Act 1991, s 22) the highway authority may agree to undertake the maintenance of a private carriage or occupation road which a person having power so to do is willing to dedicate as a highway, or any way to be constructed by a person who proposes so to dedicate it, and any such road will then become a highway maintainable at the public expense, on a date specified in the agreement (see *Porter* (1983) LS Gaz 1476). A precedent for such an Agreement can be found at Appendix 1.

11 Survey and recording

The National Parks and Access to the Countryside Act 1949 made several procedural, or 'machinery', changes in the law relating to public rights of way, some of which have already been mentioned. Perhaps the most important provisions were those requiring a survey of footpaths and bridleways, followed by a recording of such ways on maps prepared by the local authority.

These surveys were carried out by the county councils; the old pre-1974 county borough councils were not subject to the duty to carry out this procedure, but after the coming into effect of the Local Government Act 1972 (on 1 April 1974) footpaths and bridleways in such areas could be subjected to the procedure.

The procedure was drastically revised by the Wildlife and Countryside Act 1981, Part III, but in order to understand the present law, it is first desirable to explain the procedure under the 1949 Act in outline.

First, however, some definitions contained in s 66 of the 1981 Act (for the most part repeating earlier statutory provisions):

(1) 'Footpath' means a highway over which the public have a right of way on foot only, other than such a highway at the side of a public road.

(2) 'Bridleway' means a highway over which the public have the following, but no other, rights of way, that is to say, a right of way on foot and a right of way on horseback or leading a horse, with or without a right to drive animals of any description along the highway. 'Horse' includes a pony, ass and mule, and 'horseback' is to be construed accordingly. A bridleway is commonly known as a 'drove way'. Any member of the public may ride a pedal cycle on a bridleway, provided he gives precedence to foot passengers: Countryside Act 1968, s 30 and 1981 Act, s 66(3).

(3) 'Byway open to all traffic' means a highway over which the public have a right of way for vehicular and all other kinds of traffic, but which is used by the public mainly for the purpose for which footpaths and bridleways are so used.

(4) 'Public path' means a highway being either a footpath or a bridleway.

(a) 1949 Act procedure

The first step under the 1949 Act procedure was for the 'survey authority' (ie the county council or the London borough council: 1981 Act, s 66 replacing provisions in the 1949 Act) to carry out a survey of all lands in their area over which a right of way was alleged to exist. They then prepared a draft map and written statement showing thereon every public path then subsisting. This had to be advertised, and landowners and others could make representations which had to be considered by the authority after a local enquiry. Then the authority were required to prepare a provisional map and statement, which was subject to rights of appeal by landowners, etc, to the local crown court. Subject to the determination of any such questions, the authority were then required to prepare a 'definitive' map and statement which was subject to question only in the High Court on the ground that some procedural requirement had not been complied with, by proceedings commenced within six weeks of the publication of the definitive map.

(b) 1981 Act procedure

The provisions contained in the 1949 Act, ss 27–35, have now all been repealed by the 1981 Act. The definitive maps and statements in force under the 1949 Act, however, do remain, in their revised version, and where there is no definitive map and statement in force for a particular area, the survey authority are required to prepare a map and statement that will serve as the definitive map and statement (1981 Act, s 55(3)). The Department of the Environment Circular 2/93 'Public Rights of Way' states that local authorities must ensure that sufficient resources are made available to meet their statutory obligations concerning the recording of public rights of way. This they must do in accordance with the Wildlife and Countryside (Definitive Maps and Statements) Regulations 1993 (SI No 12) made by the Secretary of State (*ibid*, s 57(2)). These regulations detail the scale and notation to be used in the preparation of the definitive maps, together with the forms to be utilised when a survey authority modify their definitive map and the nature of the application which should be submitted by a person seeking a modification to the definitive map.

In accordance with the Wildlife and Countryside Act 1981 (Commencement No 6) Order 1983 (SI No 20) the survey authority must make any modifications to the definitive map and statement that are necessary by reason of any event whereby a highway has been authorised to be stopped up, diverted, widened or extended, or where a highway has ceased to be a highway of a particular description shown in the definitive map and statement, or where a new public path has been created (1981 Act, s 53(2), (3)(*a*)). A modification order must also be made (under s 53(2), (3)(*b*), (*c*)) in consequence of the discovery of evidence showing that a right of way not shown on the definitive map and statement subsists, or is reasonably alleged to subsist, or that a highway so shown ought to be shown as being of a different description, or that there is no public right of way over land shown in the map and statement as a highway.

This procedure was considered by the High Court in *Shears Court (West Mersea) Management Co Ltd v Essex CC* (1987) 85 LGR 479. Judge Prosser QC determined that it was a vexatious use of the process of law for the owners of land to seek a declaration concerning an alleged right of way, whilst the survey authority was engaged in making an order under s 53(2)(*a*). Therefore, the learned judge struck out the property owner's action.

(c) Orders under section 53(3)(*b*) or (*c*)

Any member of the public may apply to the survey authority for an order under these provisions (but *not* under subsection (3)(*a*)). The application must be made in accordance with the above regulations made by the Secretary of State, and accompanied by a map showing the way in question, and also by copies of any documentary evidence, including any statements of witnesses. A notice must also be served by the applicant on all landowners and occupiers affected, and he must certify to the authority that he has done this.

The authority must consider any application under these provisions and investigate the matter. When they have come to a decision (ie to make or not to make the required modification to the definitive map and statement), they must notify the applicant accordingly. If no notification is given within 12 months, the applicant may make representations to the Secretary of State, who may then direct the authority to determine the application (note: the Parliamentary Commissioner for Administration, commonly known as the Ombudsman, has found the Department of the Environment guilty of maladministration for failing to act with sufficient vigour and speed in deciding whether to make a direction to an authority, case C 511/91 (3 June 1992) reported in *Footpath Worker*, Vol 13 No 3 p 14). If the authority decide not to make the required modification, the applicant may, within 28 days after service on him of the notice of the authority's determination, appeal to the Secretary of State who may, if he considers that a modification order should be made, give appropriate directions to the authority (1981 Act, s 53(5) and Sched 14).

In a case where a determination is arrived at to the effect that no modification order should be made, there is no provision for a local inquiry or any right of appeal to the courts, but a decision of the Secretary of State could be called into question on an application for judicial review under RSC Ord 53 (and note *O'Reilly v Mackman* [1983] 2 AC 237): *see R v Secretary of State for the Environment, ex parte Simms* (1990), below p 28.

When a modification order is made under subs s (*b*) or (*c*), this will be subject to the procedure of Sched 15 (s 53(6)). The survey authority must consult with local authorities (district and parish or community councils and parish meetings), and the order must be publicised as prescribed in Sched 4 of the 1993 regulations (SI No 12), which invite representations or objections to be made within a period of not less than 42 days. If there are no such representations or objections the authority may confirm the order without modification and it will then come into effect. If valid objections or representations have been made and have not been withdrawn, or if any modification needs to be made to the order, the order must be referred to the Secretary of State, who will consider whether or not the order should be confirmed, after convening a local enquiry or ordering a private hearing before an inspector appointed by him. In some cases the inspector will be authorised to determine the case on behalf of the Secretary of State; in others, the Secretary of State will decide after considering the inspector's report. The order of the survey authority will only come into effect if confirmed, with or without modification, by the Secretary of State (or the inspector on his behalf), and then only after notices to that effect have been served as specified in Sched 15. Additional comments on this procedure and advice as to the tactics that may be employed by applicants have been given by *Pearlman* [1984] JPL 176. Also, the Department of the Environment provides guidance as to the awarding of costs incurred during enquiries (Circular 8/93). The normal expectation is that parties at enquiries should meet their own costs irrespective of the outcome of the proceedings. However, parties may have costs awarded against them by the Secretary of State if he considers that they have behaved 'unreasonably'. An example of unreasonable behaviour is where objectors persist with a legally irrelevant objection which obviously has no prospect of success.

Any person aggrieved by an order modifying a definitive map and statement that has taken effect may apply to the High Court for an order to quash that modification order generally, or in so far only as it affects the applicant, if he can show that it was not within the powers given by the Act, or that the requirements of Sched 15 have not been complied with. Such an application must be made within 42 days of publication of the notice of confirmation of the order (Sched 15, para 12).

The High Court has ruled that the effect of this provision is to exclude its ordinary jurisdiction to engage in judicial review of the process of making a purportedly unlawful modification order. Therefore, the court could not entertain an application from persons who sought to challenge an allegedly unlawful order prior to the order being confirmed by the Secretary of State (*R v Cornwall County Council, ex p Huntington* [1992] 3 All ER 566). A successful application under this provision was made by the Ramblers' Association in *Rubenstein v Secretary of State for the Environment* (1989) 57 P & CR 111. Taylor J (as he then was) held that s 53(3)(c)(iii) did not apply to retrospective claims by landowners that mistakes had been made in the past when compiling definitive maps. However, the Court of Appeal has unanimously overruled this interpretation in the case of *R v Secretary of State for the Environment, ex p Simms* [1990] 3 All ER 490. Simms sought to challenge the refusal of the Secretary of State to question the decision of Buckinghamshire County Council to refrain from deleting two bridleways included in the Buckinghamshire definitive map, which Simms asserted had been included through an administrative error. After reviewing the legislative history of s 53 and dicta of Lord Diplock in *Suffolk County Council v Mason* [1979] 2 All ER 369, which had not been referred to by Taylor J in *Rubinstein*, the Court of Appeal determined that s 53 required surveying authorities to ensure that their maps and statements were kept up to date. Where evidence became available that there was an error in a definitive map, or any subsequent revision of the map, the surveying authority was under a duty to revise the map and statement accordingly. As to the relationship between s 53 and s 56 (above p 31) Purchas LJ stated:

There is no difficulty in reconciling ss 53 and 56 of the 1981 Act once the comparatively restricted purpose of the legislation as a whole is understood, namely the preparation and maintenance of an authoritative record in the form of a definitive map and statement showing those highways over which the public have rights of way whether as 'ramblers' only or as 'ramblers and riders' . . . Once prepared, however, and until subsequently revised, the map and statement is to be conclusive evidence in rights of way disputes between landowners and the various categories of persons exercising rights of way. Parliament never removed the duty to revise and keep the record up to date, so that not only changes of status caused by supervening events, eg the stopping up of a highway under statute or otherwise, or the creation of prescriptive rights, but also changes in the original status of highways or even their existence resulting from recent research or discovery of evidence should all be taken into account in order to produce the most reliable map and statement that could be achieved.

In this process the passage of time still has a part to play, not by way of perpetuating errors but by refining and updating the evidential content of the map and statement. Clearly, with the passage of time, 'events' within s 53(3)(*c*) will become less and less frequent.

However, when they do occur, full cognisance of the result must be taken whether by addition under s 53(3)(*c*)(i), adjustments under sub-para (ii) or deletion under sub-para (iii). In this way equal weight can be given to the three sub-paragraphs of s 53(3)(*c*) and a strained construction avoided (at p 510).

Therefore, Simms' appeal was upheld. Commenting upon this

important case, the head of legal services for a local authority has observed that

the *Simms* decision should be welcomed by local authorities as the position under *Rubinstein* effectively had the result that a local authority could unwittingly create public paths as well as recording them (G R Chesman [1990] JPL 613).

It has also become clear that *Simms* can be invoked to 'upgrade' a right of way (eg from a footpath to a bridleway in *R v Devon County Council, ex p Fowler* [1991] JPL 520) as well as to 'downgrade' such a way.

In 1990 the Department of the Environment issued a circular (17/90) providing guidance to local authorities on the implications of *Simms*. The circular stresses that the burden of proof, that a definitive map is inaccurate, is on the applicant seeking a modification. The evidence needed to remove a right of way recorded on a definitive map will need to be cogent and as the rigorous process for recording such routes has been in operation for over 40 years it is unlikely that there are still large numbers of mistakes contained in the authoritative records. Local authorities are advised to consult widely when evaluating challenges to recorded rights of way, to ensure that all relevant evidence is fully considered. The department believes that the objective of the 1981 Act is to obtain maps and statements of the greatest accuracy and not to diminish public access to the countryside.

What amounts to 'evidence' for the purposes of s 53(3)(*c*) has been determined by the High Court in *Margaret Mayhew v Secretary of State for the Environment* (1993) 65 P & CR 344. There, Hampshire County Council had made a modification order reclassifying three footpaths as by-ways open to all traffic. The council relied upon existing evidence (primarily early 19th-century maps), which had not been considered when the definitive map had been drawn up. The order was confirmed by the Secretary of State after the holding of an enquiry. The applicant sought to challenge the order claiming, *inter alia*, that the word 'evidence' meant fresh evidence which had not existed at the time of the drawing-up or earlier reviewing of the definitive map. However, Potts J held that 'evidence' in s 53(3)(*c*) should be given its full and natural meaning; therefore, the council and the Secretary of State were entitled to have regard to the existing historical information concerning the three rights of way in issue.

(d) Orders under section 53(2) and (3)(*a*)

Under the 1981 Act such orders will take effect as soon as they have been made and do not require confirmation (s 53(6)).

(e) Duties of a survey authority

Apart from their duty to consider as soon as reasonably practicable after the appointed day whether to make a modification order as above described, the authority are also under a duty:

(1) To keep the definitive map and statement under continuous review and to make modification orders as and when may appear to them to be requisite (1981 Act, s 53(2)(*b*)).

(2) As soon as reasonably practicable after the appointed day to carry out a review of such particulars in the definitive map and statement as relate to roads used as public paths (this is an expression which first appeared in the statute book in the Countryside Act 1968, since repealed, without definition) and to make appropriate modification orders reclassifying such roads as by-ways open to all traffic, as bridleways, or as footpaths (1981 Act, s 54). The provisions of Sched 15 to the Act, as described above, will apply to any such modification order (s 54(1)). This process has received judicial scrutiny by the High Court in *Lasham Parish Meeting v Hampshire County Council* (1993) 91 LGR 209. There the surveying authority had made a modification order concerning a road used as a public path in the Parish of Lasham which the authority considered to be a by-way open to all traffic. The Parish Meeting was consulted about the order and (advised by Lord Denning) objected that the by-way was unsuited to vehicular traffic. The authority responded that this was a legally irrelevant matter in the reclassification process and, therefore, proceeded to confirm the modification as an unopposed order. Subsequently the Parish Meeting applied to the High Court to have the order quashed on the grounds that it was not within the powers of s 54 and Sched 15 had not been complied with. Potts LJ upheld the surveying authority's construction of s 54, that it did not permit such authorities to consider matters of suitability and amenity when undertaking the reclassification of roads used as public paths.

Section 54 merely gives the surveying authority the power to decide which of the three descriptions specified in subs (2) should apply to the way in question given the requirements of subs (3). Accordingly, if a public right of way for vehicular traffic has been shown to exist, the way must be reclassified as a byway open to all traffic. This is entirely consistent with the purpose of this part of the Act, which is to ascertain what rights exist, not what rights ought to or should exist (at p 216).

However, Potts LJ agreed with the applicant's contention that provided an objection is made within the requisite time limits and in the manner prescribed by the order, the objection must be referred to the Secretary of State for his confirmation (even where the objection is based upon legally irrelevant grounds). Therefore, the surveying authority ought not to have confirmed the order itself, however his Lordship concluded that as the applicant's objection was bound to be rejected by the Secretary of State, the order should not be quashed. Any way so re-classified will become a highway maintainable at the public expense, and so it will be the duty of the survey authority, as highway authority, to keep it in reasonable repair (see p 53 and s 54(4)), but this does not mean that a by-way open to all traffic must necessarily be maintained in a state suitable for the passage of vehicles, nor does it prevent a traffic regulation order being made in respect thereof under the Road Traffic Regulation Act 1984 (s 54(7)).

(3) To prepare a map and statement to serve as a definitive map and statement, where none exists for the area as above stated, or if so directed by the Secretary of State, to complete a survey; but otherwise no new survey is to be undertaken under the 1949 Act (1981 Act, s 55).

(4) Further, by s 57, the authority must keep a copy of the definitive map and statement (and any modification orders) available for inspection by members of the public at all reasonable hours free of charge in each parish. They must also take steps to bring the existence of the definitive map and statement to the notice of the public.

(5) Finally, every order modifying a definitive map and statement must specify the 'relevant date' for the purposes of the order, this being a date not earlier than six months before the making of the order (s 56(3)).

(f) Effect of the definitive map and statement

The definitive map and statement is conclusive evidence as to particulars therein to the following extent (see s 56(1) and *Simms* p 28):

(1) where the map shows a footpath, that there was at the relevant
    date (ie the date specified in the statement or in any relevant
    orders: s 56(2)) a highway as shown over which the public
    had a right of way on foot (for the application of this provision
    in a criminal prosecution see *Lancashire CC v Clarke* (1984)
    148 JP 656);

(2) where the map shows a bridleway, that there was at the
    relevant date a highway as shown on the map over which the
    public had a right of way on horseback or leading a horse;

(3) where the map shows a by-way open to all traffic, that at the
    relevant date the public had a right of way for vehicles and
    all other kinds of traffic; and

(4) where the map shows a road used as a public path, that there
    was at the relevant date a highway as shown over which the
    public had a right of way on foot or on horseback, or leading
    a horse.

In each of these cases, the provision is without prejudice to proof
that the public also had any further right of way over the highway
in question. The conclusive presumption can of course be altered
by a modification order as described above, possibly initiated by a
member of the public, and such an order can even delete from the
map a right of way shown thereon. Section 56 seems also to preserve
the position under the former section, s 32 of the 1949 Act, whereby
it may be established (and not only by way of a modification order,
but perhaps by a declaration made by the court) that there is a right
of way over land where none is shown on the definitive map and
statement. This was accepted under the 1949 Act in the county
court case of *Andover Corporation v Mundy* [1955] JPL 518.

The decision of the House of Lords in *Suffolk CC v Mason* [1979]
AC 705, in which it was held that the appearance on the map and
statement of a way as 'footpath' was conclusive, and could not be
elevated to a bridleway by new evidence is clearly now no longer
law in view of the express terms of s 56(1).

Section 56 also provides that any particulars in the statement as
to the width or position of the way are to be conclusive evidence,
as are any statements as to conditions or limitations affecting the
rights of the public, but without prejudice to any question whether
at a precise date the right of way was subject to any other conditions
or limitations.

(g) Conclusion

Members of the public can thus question the status (footpath, bridle-way, etc) of a public right of way, whether one should be shown on the definitive map when it is not so shown, or indeed question the correctness of a way being shown at all, by:

(1) applying for a modification order, at any time; *or*
(2) applying to the High Court for a declaration, except in the case where it is desired to challenge the existence of a public path as shown on the map.

In any such proceedings, and when the survey authority are considering whether to make a modification order, or the Secretary of State (or his inspector) is considering whether to confirm an order, the ordinary rules of the common law as to the existence, etc, of a right of way, as discussed in this book will apply, subject only to the procedural restrictions of the 1981 Act.

It is also worth remembering that, in certain circumstances, an application to divert or stop up an existing right of way may achieve the objective of challenging a right of way; as to which see Chapter 6, p 75.

Chapter 3

The Creation of Public Rights of Way by Long Use

1 Introduction

As previously stated (see p 14), the Prescription Act 1832 does not apply to the acquisition of a *public* right of way, and therefore, at common law, user had to be established on the basis either of a presumed dedication and acceptance by the public, or of actual user back to the limits of legal memory, ie, 1189. Prior to the Rights of Way Act 1932 'it was extremely doubtful whether a public right of way could be acquired by prescription and, generally speaking, it is true to say that the only way in which a public right of way could be created, apart from express creation of statute, was by dedication by the owner of the soil' (*per* Farwell J in *Jones v Bates* [1938] 2 All ER 237, at p 251).

However, the Rights of Way Act 1932 (now repealed) established a virtually indefeasible right, to be put into practice by uninterrupted public user over a period of 20 years. The provisions of that Act were replaced by ss 34–36 of the Act of 1959, now ss 31–33 of the Highways Act 1980. The most important of these provisions is s 31(1):

Where a way over any land [an expression which includes, for this purpose, land covered with water: 1980 Act, s 31(11); see p 36], other than a way of such a character that use of it by the public could not give rise at common law to any presumption of dedication, has been actually enjoyed by the public as of right and without interruption for a full period of 20 years, the way is to be deemed to have been dedicated as a highway unless there is sufficient evidence that there was no intention during that period to dedicate it.

These sections are in no sense rendered obsolete by Part III of the 1981 Act. Although the definitive map and statement is conclusive evidence of the existence of a right of way at a relevant date, evidence may still be adduced to show that a public right of way subsists where none is shown on the map.

2 Comments on the Highways Act 1980, s 31(1)

Under this provision, if user in the conditions prescribed is proved to the satisfaction of the tribunal of fact, a statutory presumption arises that the way has been dedicated by the owner of the soil. This point was expressed by Scott LJ in *Jones v Bates* (above), at p 246:

The change of the law is that, upon proof of such a user for 20 years, the conclusion of dedication follows as a presumption *juris et de jure*, instead of as an inference of fact to be drawn by the tribunal of fact.

For a case where a claim succeeded under the Act where the facts would not have justified a case at common law, see *Att-Gen and Newton Abbot Rural District Council v Dyer* [1947] Ch 67.

It would seem that this procedure does not supersede the common law method of establishing a public right of way by proof of dedication and user, but there are judicial dicta to the contrary. Scott LJ in *Jones v Bates*, at p 247 said: 'If what I have said is correct, the Act applies to all future disputes after 1 January 1934 when the [Rights of Way Act 1932] came into force and there is no longer a common-law procedure for establishing the public right outside the statute.' The learned lord justice came to this conclusion by interpreting the word 'full' in the subsection as meaning 'at least'. In the same case, at p 251, Farwell J in a dissenting judgment, said:

In my judgment, notwithstanding the Act of 1932, it is still true to say that, apart from statute, dedication is the only way by which a right of way can be created. It is still possible to prove the existence of such a right where the existence is less than twenty years, but where the user is for twenty years or more, no implication is necessary because in that event [the Act] provides that there shall be deemed to have been dedication, if during that period dedication would have been possible.

Moreover, this judgment of Scott LJ ignores the provisions of s 31(9) (see p 47), and in *Att-Gen and Newton Abbot Rural District Council v Dyer* (above), Evershed J held that the plaintiffs were entitled to rely on the Act although it was not pleaded, and that, had the plaintiffs' case depended on their alternative claim at common law, it would have failed. Generally, this case illustrates the importance of ensuring that the proceedings are accurately pleaded so as to include all possible claims relying on both statutes and common law. It is now proposed to consider the precise wording of the section in detail.

(a) 'A way over any land'

This phrase was defined by the House of Lords in the *Yorkshire Derwent Trust* case (see above p 8). In that case their Lordships noted that subs 1(8), now subs 31(11X), provided that ' "land" includes land covered with water'. Whilst expressing some uncertainty as to the intention of the draftsman the elaboration was given the following meaning:

'I can think of no other purpose for the addition of this subsection than ex abunddanti cautela to counteract any argument, however ill-founded, that a way which runs, for instance, through a ford, is not a way "upon or over land" or that the periods of 20 and 40 years are to be considered as interrupted because the site of the way is covered, either permanently or temporarily, by water.' (*per* Lord Oliver at pp 247–248)

In addition this phrase includes a way over water by a bridge or stepping stones; see the definition of 'land' in s 329(1) of the 1980 Act. A bridge carrying the highway is part of the highway: s 328(2).

(b) 'Other than a way of such a character that use of it by the public could not give rise at common law to any presumption of dedication'

These words cover every sort of conditional user by the public; and it must be remembered that mere public user does not create a highway. The law has always recognised that the foundation of public rights lies in dedication; and dedication presumes a dedicator. That dedicator can only be the fee simple owner of the land over which the right of way has been granted. In the absence of any definite proof of actual and deliberate dedication (whether by statute, gift, agreement or otherwise) the courts have adopted the legal fiction of assuming dedication from the proved facts; by this section there is a legal presumption of dedication if user in accordance with the subsection, and subject to the provisos indicated, is proved. For examples of alleged dedication, see *Healey v Batley Corporation* (1875) 39 JP 423; *Hall v Bootle Corporation* (1881) 44 LT 873; *Webb v Baldwin* (1911) 75 JP 564; and *Folkestone Corporation v Brockman* [1914] AC 338. As to the nature of user, and the weight to be given to evidence of it, see the judgment of Lord Kinnear in the last-mentioned case, quoted in *Merstham Manor Ltd v Coulsdon and Purley Urban District Council* [1937] 2 KB 77 and set out fully on p 95.

(c) 'As of right'

This excludes any suggestion of permission by the owner to use the way; and inasmuch as many paths have more or less tacitly been used by the public, though the owner has merely granted the use to a limited number of persons, eg his own employees, or visitors to a neighbouring hotel, it may well be that the evidence of user by all sorts of people for the period of 20 years may be rebutted by showing absence of intention to dedicate to the public: see p 41.

For other cases on the words 'as of right', see *R v St Benedict Cambridge* (1821) 4 B & Ald 447; *Harper v Charlesworth* (1825) 4 B & C 574 (user to be open and known to owners); *Brackley v Midland Railway Co* (1916) 80 JP 369; and *Gloucestershire CC v Farrow* [1985] 1 WLR 741.

In *Merstham Manor Ltd v Coulsdon and Purley Urban District Council* (*above*) Hilbery J after pointing out that the words 'actually enjoyed by the public as of right' were reproduced from the language of the Prescription Act 1832, quoted from the judgment of Lindley LJ in *Hollins v Verney* (1884) 13 QBD, at pp 308, 309, as being specially applicable, and 'as involving that he who asserts the right must establish as a matter of fact on the one hand the actual enjoyment of the right by the public as of right, and on the other hand the actual suffering of exercise of that right by the landowner for the full period of 20 years', taking the word 'enjoyed' to mean 'having had the amenity or advantage of using' (per Kay LJ in *Cooper v Straker* (1888) 40 ChD 21). Referring to the meaning of the qualification 'as of right' the learned judge cited the judgment of Brett LJ in *Earl de la Warr v Miles* (1881) 17 ChD, at p 591, which appeared to require that the quality of the acts as well as the acts themselves must be established. The essential quality of the acts was, he thought, indicated by Cotton LJ *ibid*, at p 596 where he said: 'You must see whether the acts have been done as of right, that is to say, not secretly, not as acts of violence, not under permission from time to time given'. As to this definition, Scott LJ in *Jones v Bates* (above), at p 245 said: 'The party asserting the right of way has not to prove the absence of compulsion, secrecy or licence. It is for the party denying the existence of the right of way to prove compulsion, secrecy or licence'. In the same case, Slessor LJ approved the dictum of Tomlin J in *Hue v Whiteley* [1929] 1 Ch 440, at p 445 where he defines the term 'as of right' as meaning that the users were 'believing themselves to be exercising a public right to pass from one highway to another'.

(d) 'And without interruption'

Note the 'and'. The claimants must prove both that the enjoyment was as of right *and* that it was without interruption. Further, the onus does not shift onto the opposing landowner at this stage. Admissions in cross-examination may suffice to negative the claimant's own case, so that it will never be sufficient to call a string of people to say that they have traversed the road for 20 years. There must be substantive evidence that the user has been as of right *and* uninterrupted.

Interruption may consist in nothing more than the closing of the pathway against all comers for a single day; or it may consist in isolated acts of 'turning back'. The interruption must be by the owner himself or by his authority. The usual method of saving ownership rights and of negativing any intention to dedicate is to close the pathway on certain days in the year with an express intimation of the reason for so doing. In some parts of the country Good Friday seems to be commonly used for this purpose, but clearly one day is no more significant than another. Indeed, closure on any day every year is not strictly necessary. One single effective interruption during the previous twenty years, left unchallenged, will suffice to defeat a public right of way claim, and it is not necessary that this should have been acquiesced in for a year (as in the case with a *private* right of way; see p 113).

What must be the nature of the interruption which the enjoyment of the way must be without? Is it sufficient to amount to an interruption if acts have from time to time been done which, while actually suffering the user to go on, yet challenged the right; or must the interruption be some physical and actual interruption which prevents the enjoyment of the way? With regard to this I can find no help in the rest of the Act, but the words themselves are used in connection with 'actual enjoyment' for a period of years. As it is actual enjoyment which must be without interruption, one would suppose that the interruption contemplated must be actual. One can scarcely interrupt acts except by some physical act which stops them. I therefore think that the word 'interruption' is properly to be construed as meaning actual and physical stopping of the enjoyment, and not that the enjoyment has been free of any acts which merely challenged the public

right to that enjoyment. In practice, this construction of the words will
lead to no difficulty and cause no surprise. Many bodies, such as the four
Inns of Court, over and through whose property run roads used by the
public, take the precaution to close and actually to stop the public enjoyment of those roads for one day at least in every year: per Hilbery J in
Merstham Manor Ltd v *Coulsdon and Purley Urban District Council* (above)
at p 85 (note: now only the Inner Temple and Middle Temple close their
gates; see Samuels (1986) Conv 161).

In *Jones v Bates* (above) Scott LJ said, at p 246:

The next requirement of the statute 'without interruption', means that the
enjoyment of the right must not have been interrupted. If for the statutory
period members of the public have used the way as of right, and their
exercise of that right has not been interrupted, then the statutory consequence follows. A mere absence of continuity in the *de facto* user will not
prevent the statute from running. If that were not so, the necessary proof
in public rights of way cases would often break down—especially in the
40-year period—simply because witnesses were not available to fill all the
gaps in such proof. No interruption comes within the statute unless it is
shown to have been an interference with the enjoyment of the right of
passage.

Any interruption *in fact* (which may not necessarily be intended
to be an interruption) is sufficient, but 'on the other hand . . . the
presence or absence of a challenge may well be a relevant circumstance in determining whether in truth there has been an interruption in fact' (*per* Evershed MR in *Lewis v Thomas* [1950] 1 KB 438,
at p 444).

(e) 'Full period of twenty years'

In *Jones* v *Bates* (above) Scott LJ interpreted the word 'full' as
meaning 'at least'. The object of this interpretation was to extend
the scope of the Act so that the common law would be completely
superseded. It may be doubted whether this interpretation was
essential for the decision in the case and *per contra*, see the remarks
of Farwell J in the same case quoted above at p 35.

By s 31(2), it is provided that the period of 20 years is to be
calculated retrospectively from the date when the right of the public
to use the way is brought into question by notice or otherwise. By
'notice' here is meant a notice posted under s 31(3) (see p 42);
'otherwise' means, presumably, any effective means of interruption.
The placing of a notice will thus assist in proving the earliest date
at which a way was blocked to public user, or at which the public
were excluded. Proof of such an occasion, not followed by any

successful challenge on the part of the public, would serve the same purpose by way of evidence as the proof of the erection of a notice.

From the point of view of the public, the same sort of evidence will suffice to support a claim of a public right of way. Thus, if a date can be fixed at which the setting up of a notice or the stopping up of the way or the turning back of the public was challenged, that is the date up to which (not *from* which) it will be necessary to give evidence of public user, and this may be before or after the passing of the 1932 Act (see *Att-Gen and Newton Abbot Rural District Council v Dyer* [1947] Ch 67). An interesting case on this point is *South Eastern Railway Co v Warr* (1923) 21 LGR 669, in which there had been continuous obstruction of the public passage for 30 years prior to the commencement of the action. Evidence was available, however, to prove the user of the way as of right by the public for a long period of years prior to the obstruction, with the result that the court found in favour of the public: see also *Williams-Ellis v Cobb* [1935] 1 KB 310.

When considering how the period of 20 years is calculated,

the thing to do is to find the finishing point and then count back 20 years . . . I think that, in order for the right of the public to have been 'brought into question', the land-owner must challenge it by some means sufficient to bring it home to the public that he is challenging their right to use the way, so that they may be apprised of the challenge and have a reasonable opportunity of meeting it: (*per* Denning LJ in *Fairey v Southampton County Council* [1956] 2 QB 439, at p 456).

For a case where the 20-year period was not established see *De Rothschild v Buckinghamshire County Council* (1957) 8 P & CR 317, from which it appears that the 20-year period need not necessarily run back from the *first* time that the public right was called into question. Nevertheless, in *R v Secretary of State for the Environment, ex p Blake* [1984] JPL 101 the plaintiff was required to prove that the route of the alleged highway had remained constant throughout the entire 20-year period.

(f) 'Is to be deemed to have been dedicated as a highway'

Subject to the conditions being satisfied, if the user for the required period is proved, there is a presumption of law that the highway has been dedicated and the court has not, as under the common law, to presume dedication as an inference of fact.

(g) 'Sufficient evidence that there was no intention during that period to dedicate'

When does rebutting evidence become necessary? Presumably not until the claimants' case has been substantively proved. It is submitted that the mere fact of uninterrupted user by individual members of the public over a period of 20 years is not sufficient to establish a *prima facie* case. Circumstances showing that the user was 'as of right' must also be forthcoming. That having been established, the freeholder must then prove affirmatively that during that period he had no intention to dedicate. The meaning of this phrase has not received judicial interpretation. Clearly it does not contemplate 'interruption', as the onus of proving 'user as of right and without interruption' is on the person affirming the right of way, and such an interpretation would be tautological. A mere assertion of non-intention would probably not be sufficient (*Barraclough v Johnson* (1838) 8 Ad & El 99), but possibly the existence of notices at the points of ingress to the way maintained during the whole of these periods would suffice to negative intention, and presumably it is necessary that the absence of intention to dedicate should be manifested in some way; but this should not be taken too far: see *per* Lord Goddard CJ in *De Rothschild v Buckinghamshire County Council* (1957) 8 P & CR 317, at p 323. Since 1932 such action or notification to the appropriate authority has certainly been sufficient to negative intention to dedicate (see s 31(3) and (5)).

Scott LJ in *Jones v Bates* (above) at p 247, appreciated the difficulty that it might be possible for the owner of the soil to show non-intention during the 20-year period, but there might be evidence of intention prior to this period. In order to overcome this difficulty and prevent the claimants having to prove their case in accordance with common law procedure in the pre-statute period, the learned Lord Justice developed an argument for extending the Act to cover all time preceding the 20 years but this is doubtful (pp 35 and 39).

3 Defences

The statutory provisions, after establishing the general principle that a public right of way may be acquired by 20 years' use, then enable the owner of the land to take certain steps if he wishes to ensure that a public right of way is not so acquired. If these steps are taken in the manner prescribed by the statute, no right of way can be established, but the procedure must be carefully followed.

(a) Notice boards

In the first place, it is provided by s 31(3) (re-enacting similar provisions in the Rights of Way Act 1932) that where the owner of land over which the way passes has erected, in such manner as to be visible to persons using the way, a notice inconsistent with the dedication of the way as a highway, and has maintained the notice after the date on which it was erected (or 1 January 1934, the date when the Rights of Way Act 1932 came into operation, whichever was the earlier), the notice shall 'in the absence of proof of a contrary intention, be sufficient evidence to negative the intention to dedicate the way as a highway'. (By s 31(7), it is provided that for the purposes of this section 'owner' is to have the special meaning of 'a person who is for the time being entitled to dispose of the fee simple in the land'. It would therefore include trustees for sale, a tenant for life for the purposes of the Settled Land Act 1925, and a mortgagee in possession.) Further (by s 31(5)), if such a notice is torn down or defaced, the owner may give a notice to the London borough council (including the Common Council of the City of London) or (as the case may be) the county council in which the way is situate, to the effect that the way is not dedicated as a highway, and this will have the same effect. The following points arise on these subsections:

(i) Erection of notice

Under s 31(4), an owner of land is given power to enter and place a notice (referred to in s 31(3)) without leave of any tenant occupying the land under a term of years or a tenancy from year to year. The landlord may not, however, cause any injury to 'the business or occupation of the tenant', or presumably otherwise unnecessarily interfere with the tenant's quiet enjoyment of the premises. Where a landlord wishes to ensure that the notice is maintained, a specific obligation should be imposed upon the tenant in the lease to make the position clear. The tenant, it may be noted, has no right to dedicate a way.

(ii) 'A notice inconsistent with the dedication'

The usual type of notice in the past has been in some such simple form as: 'Trespassers will be prosecuted'. Many of these notices may still be found, and many of them will have been in existence for more than 20 years. Such ancient notice boards will be of great value as evidence; and though they will not be conclusive, it will be difficult to prove contrary intention where the existence of such notice is proved. A notice couched in these terms must, however, be placed in such a position that it clearly relates to passage along a defined way. In the interests of accuracy, however, this wording is to be deprecated, as civil proceedings only can be taken in respect of trespass, unless some special statute authorises criminal proceedings (eg the Public Order Act 1986, s 39, which was enacted to deal with the type of mass trespass committed by some members of the annual Stonehenge convoy). Ambiguous notices, such as 'No Through Way' and 'Private Road' also should be avoided; 'No Public Right of Way' should be preferred. There are numerous instances in which direction posts have been erected for the convenience of visitors to places of interest on private property indicating which of several roadways leads to the desired spot. The roadway indicated may, nevertheless, be private, and it does not follow that the direction post indicates that the roadway is public. It will, however, obviously be to the owner's interest when erecting such a direction post (or allowing it to be erected) to have it clearly described as a private road; and, for his own more complete protection, to cause it to be closed at least one day in the year. See p 38 and subpara (d) (below).

(iii) 'Visible to persons using the way'

It is essential that such a notice shall be 'visible'. Many of these ancient notice boards require some little effort to decipher, but the fact of the board being visible, and even more so that the fact that the word 'notice' can generally be read without much effort, is sufficient to call the attention of persons using the way. It is submitted that the very existence of such a board should put passers-by on their guard and place on them the onus of ascertaining whether there is any public right of way. 'Visible' is not the same thing as 'legible'. A person unable to read may yet see a notice board and so be put on inquiry. It will also be observed that the expression 'persons using the way' contemplates the use of ways by persons who may not be entitled to do so—in other words, it impliedly recalls the fact that it is not *user* by the public but the *intention of the owner* that is the foundation of any right of way (see p 14).

(iv) 'Proof of a contrary intention'

This phrase appears to contemplate the possibility of proof being forthcoming of conduct on the part of an owner inconsistent with the notice exhibited on the way. Such conduct must, however, be of such a character as to negative the intention to maintain the privacy of the way: and mere failure to challenge persons occasionally using it is not necessarily inconsistent with the intention of the owner to maintain the privacy. It would require some definite act, such as the removal of the notice board by the owner, to show a definite intention to dedicate. Although there may be a duty on the highway authority to erect sign posts (Countryside Act 1968, s 27 as amended by s 65 of the 1981 Act, see p 51), it does not of necessity follow that a sign post is proof of a public right of way. Many sign posts have been erected by landowners, or by their permission, in order to guide persons having lawful business on their estates or otherwise. Thus a farm occupation road or driftway may have a sign post indicating the route to a particular farm or grazing ground. This does not of necessity imply that the road indicated is a highway. In cases of that sort it may be very important to be able to prove in evidence when and by whom the sign post was erected. Similarly, the fact that a landlord has allowed the local authority to do repairs to a roadway, though suggestive of public rights, is by no means conclusive. On the other hand, the fact that the local authority have never done repairs to a roadway is strong presumptive evidence that it is not a public highway. See p 48 as to liability for repairs generally.

(v) 'Torn down or defaced'

This provision should operate to make unnecessary the time-honoured practice of stopping-up by the owners and breaking up by the public which has so often led to a breach of the peace. Once a notice board is torn down or defaced, all that the owner needs to do is to send formal notice of the fact to the local authority with an intimation that the way is not dedicated to the public. The onus will then be upon the authority to take action (as guardians of public rights of way) in pursuance of the general duty of the authority to assert and protect the rights of the public, under the Highways Act 1980, s 130(3). They may obtain a declaration from the county court, or make a modification order to the definitive map and statement under the 1981 Act (see p 25). Failing such action, the written notice served on them by the landowner will hold good. It may, however, be desirable, in the owner's interest, to follow this action by a further notice. It is submitted that no amount of user by the public after service of a written 'defacement' notice followed by the prescribed action under s 31(6) will suffice to displace the owner's contention: and therefore the local authority will have to take action or allow the public claim to fail by default.

(vi) 'The appropriate council'

The notice required under the subsection should be addressed to the authority and left at, or sent by post to, the principal office of the authority (Local Government Act 1972, s 231). In the area covered by the former Greater London Council any such notice should be sent to the London borough concerned or, within the City, to the Common Council of the City (s 31(7)).

(vii) Temporary, conditional or occasional use

It should be observed that, although a landowner may intend to preserve his rights to the full by not allowing a pathway or roadway to become public, he is in no way prejudiced if he grants temporary, conditional or occasional use by the public. In such a case any notices exhibited should be carefully drafted.

(b) Maps and statements

Whether or not a notice has been erected *in situ* under s 31(3), the owner of land affected may (as an alternative or additionally) deposit with the council of the county or the London borough or Common Council of the City of London:
  (1) a map to a scale of not less than six inches to one mile, showing land owned by him; and
  (2) a statement indicating which ways (if any) over that land he admits to have been dedicated as highways.
(For method of service of such documents, see above, para f). Such a map and statement should then be reinforced at least every six years with a statutory declaration made by the owner or his successors in title and lodged with the same council, to the effect that no additional way (other than any specifically indicated in the

declaration) over the land delineated on the map has been dedicated as a highway since the date of deposit or the previous statutory declaration (as the case may be). In any case where such a map and statement, and declarations (where appropriate), have been duly deposited, in the absence of any contrary intention (see p 41), this will be deemed to be sufficient evidence (see p 93) to negative the intention of the owner or his successors in title to dedicate any such additional way as a highway (s 31(6)).

This section provides a means whereby the landowner can obtain some safeguards against future encroachments, but it has not been widely used in practice. Since local authorities carried out their surveys of public paths under the National Parks and Access to the Countryside Act 1949 (see p 24), the section has become very largely obsolete.

It will be open to 'any person interested' to inspect these maps, statements and statutory declarations at the offices of the local authority at all reasonable hours for a charge of 10p, with an extra charge of 10p for each hour that the inspection continues after the first hour (Local Government Act 1972, s 228(5), read with s 225).

Similarly, the definitive map and statement and any modification orders made by the surveying authority relating to public rights of way under the 1981 Act (see s 57(5) of that Act) must be made available for public inspection at the offices of the local authority at all reasonable hours at appropriate places in each district and parish.

4 General observations

Primarily, action can be taken under the Highways Act 1980, s 31(3) only by the owner (see definition on p 42) of the land over which the way passes, but a reversioner immediately expectant upon the determination of a tenancy for life (or *pur autre vie*), although under the 1925 property legislation entitled only to an equitable interest in the land, is given by s 33 remedies by action for trespass or an injunction to prevent the acquisition by the public of a right of way over the land as if he were in possession thereof. He is not in all respects in the same position as an owner, because he cannot erect a notice under s 31(3) or deposit a map and statement under s 31(6).

Acquisition of a right of way by use over 20 years is the normal method established by the section (and its predecessor), but this does not mean that the existence of a public right of way cannot be established by any other method. As we have seen (see p 17), express dedication creates a public right of way, and a dedication will be presumed from the intention of the owner followed by acceptance by the public; use over a period of years may be merely one element in establishing such intention and acceptance (see *Folkestone Corporation v Brockman* [1914] AC 338; and p 95). These legal principles have been preserved expressly by s 31(9) of the 1980 Act, which provides that nothing in the section shall operate to prevent the dedication of a way as a highway being presumed on proof of user for any less period than 20 years, or being presumed or proved in any circumstances in which it might have been presumed or proved before the passing of the Act.

A limited company or corporate body may dedicate a right of way to public use so long as there are no provisions in the relevant statute, memorandum of association, trust deed or other document defining the powers of the body which would make such dedication *ultra vires*. In particular, if such dedication would be inconsistent with the main purpose of the body in question, such dedication will be presumed to be *ultra vires* in the absence of an express power: see *R v Inhabitants of Leake* (1833) 5 B & Ad 469; *Grand Junction Hotel Co v Petty* (1888) 21 QBD 273; and *British Transport Commission v Westmorland County Council* [1958] AC 126. The position of such corporate bodies is not affected by s 31, by virtue of subs (8). As to evidence in right of way cases, see p 93.

Chapter 4

The Repair and Maintenance of Public Rights of Way

1 Introduction

Disputes may arise between local authorities and owners or occupiers of land as to the repair of stiles and gateways and the general maintenance of roadways and footpaths in such a condition that the public are not incommoded in the exercise of their rights of user.

The repair of public footpaths stands on the same basis as the repair of any other highways. The law is now contained in the Highways Act 1980, s 41 (replacing in the same terms the Highways Act 1959, s 44(1)), which imposes an express duty on the highway authority to maintain any highway (of any kind) that is maintainable at the public expense. In order to ascertain which highways are in law so maintainable one must study the older statute.

As a general principle, at common law all highways were repairable by 'the inhabitants at large'. This very ancient law was founded on the theory that the inhabitants of each parish should assume the duty of keeping their own roadways in repair as consideration for their enjoying the privilege of using all the public roads in the realm (see judgment of Parke B in *R v Inhabitants of Leake* (1833) 5 B & Ad 469).

In the absence, therefore, of any statutory or other provision, the responsibility for doing surface repairs to rights of way of all kinds rested at common law upon the inhabitants of the particular parish. However, this liability was abolished by s 38(1) of the Act of 1959, and s 44(1) was enacted in its place; the 1959 position was preserved by the 1980 Act, s 36. Further, these sections, which replace s 47 of the National Parks and Access to the Countryside Act 1949, apply the general rule to all public footpaths created after 16 December 1949. Ways formerly classified as roads used as public paths, and reclassified (as footpaths, bridleways or byways open to all traffic) by modification orders made under s 54 of the 1981 Act, are maintainable at the public expense (1981 Act, s 54(4)). As a consequence of changes in the law made by the Local Government Act 1972, s 187 (and see s 1(2) of the Act of 1980), this means that (in so far as public paths are concerned) the county councils are responsible for maintenance but district councils have an option to undertake such maintenance. The liability to repair and replace stiles and gateways is discussed below (see p 56).

In the case of roads, regard also must be had to the Highway Act 1835, s 23. This provided that no roadway made after 20 March 1836 at the expense of any individual or private person or corporate body, nor any road already set out or to be set out as a private driftway or horsepath in any award under an Inclosure Act should be deemed to be a highway repairable by the inhabitants of the parish, unless the person or corporate body proposing to dedicate it to the use of the public conformed to certain conditions, *inter alia*, as to giving notice to the local surveyor (now the highway authority) and as to making up the roadway of a prescribed width and in a substantial manner to the satisfaction of the inhabitants assembled in vestry and to the approval of two justices.

The 1835 Act gave rise to a remarkable state of affairs which has continued up to the present time. Section 38 of the 1959 Act gave a list of various categories of highways 'maintainable at the public expense' which were (by s 44(1)) therefore maintainable by the highway authority, but the previous law was in effect kept in operation by virtue of these provisions, as the first category was 'a highway which immediately before the commencement of this Act was maintainable by the inhabitants at large of any area'. (See now ss 36(1) and 41(1) of the 1980 Act.) Where, after the passing of the 1835 Act, a landowner was prepared to grant leave to the public to pass over his land, he saw no reason why he should enter upon formalities under the Act which would involve a great deal of trouble and only end in a demand that he should add to his gift of a right of way a substantial sum for the cost of making a roadway to satisfy the public upon whom he was conferring a favour. Consequently, the procedural provisions of s 23 of the 1835 Act became almost a dead letter. Only those landowners acted upon it who had particular interests of their own to serve in so doing. Others simply did nothing but allowed the public to make 'short cuts' over their land, without undertaking for themselves or exacting from the users any conditions as to repairing and maintaining the tracks thus created. That is the explanation of the existence today of public roadways for the repair of which nobody is legally responsible.

Public paths are not affected by the 1835 Act provision, and paths at the side of roads not laid out as such are not 'highways' for the purpose of the Highway Act 1835, and so are subject to the common law rule when they are highways in fact: *Robinson v Richmond (Surrey) Borough Council* [1955] 1 QB 401, explained in *Margate Corporation v Roach* [1960] 1 WLR 1380.

2 'Nobody's liability'

The principal effect of the Highway Act 1835, s 23 therefore, was to bring to an end the state of affairs which had hitherto existed under the common law, *viz*, that whenever a roadway was dedicated (either expressly or by implication) to the public, and accepted by the public as a highway, the inhabitants of each parish through which it ran were liable to keep it in repair so far as their own area was concerned. Where townships arose absorbing several parishes they generally acquired by custom or statute the liability of all—a matter which, however, it is not necessary to pursue here in detail.

When the question arises, therefore, as to whose liability it is to repair a public roadway, the first question to ask is: was it in existence and repairable by the inhabitants prior to 20 March 1836? If it was, the old common law liability remains and the roadway is known as 'an ancient highway', now maintainable at the public expense (*Sorensen v Cheshire CC* (1980) 44 J Crim L 4). If not— then we must look elsewhere for the elements that fix responsibility. Many important legal results depend upon this distinction—quite apart from the fixing of liability to repair. For example, under Pt XI of the Act of 1980, the county council may be able to compel frontagers to pay for the cost of 'making-up' (ie paving, sewering, etc) streets; but they can fix the responsibility for this only upon owners of premises fronting, adjoining or abutting on streets which are not highways maintainable at the public expense. (Similar observations apply where the street is being made up under the corresponding provisions of some local legislation.) If the frontagers can bring the road within the protection of the old statute they may be able to escape liability for such road charges. 'Down to the year 1835,' said Wills J in *Eyre v New Forest Highway Board* (1892) 56 JP 517, 'if you establish that there was a public right of way, liability to repair followed'. The learned judge in the same case set out the test quite clearly:

Up till the year 1835 when the Highway Act was passed, if there was a dedication of a road to the public by the owner, *either expressed by deed* (as occasionally happens) *or inferred by public user* . . . sufficient to found the inference that he had said so or had so conducted himself as to imply that he had granted that right of passage to the public *and the public had on their part accepted and used the right*, from that moment there was not only the right of passage on the part of the public but there was also the liability to repair on the part of the parish.

Proof is required, therefore, in such a case that the roadway in question had been the subject of dedication by the owner and of acceptance by the public. How that can be proved or controverted will be seen on reference to p 93 et seq, where the subject of evidence is dealt with.

It may therefore happen that the liability to repair a road across a field or a carriageway running through private property cannot be fixed upon anybody. This is the explanation of many complaints as to driftways and roadways being impassable; and it often results in private individuals who own the subsoil and suffer inconvenience, in common with the public, doing repairs for their own comfort. This does not (see below) render them liable to continue to do so— nor if repairs are done at any time by the local authority does that act of itself fix future liability upon the local authority (see p 53). There are, however, certain circumstances in which private individuals may become liable to do repairs; and similarly, there are ways in which local authorities may assume responsibility where the road or way has not been formally adopted. Thus, a district, parish or community council *may* undertake the maintenance of a footpath or bridleway under the Highways Act 1980, s 50.

3 Liability of adjoining owners or occupiers

Even in the case of a public right of way in existence prior to 20 March 1836 it is sometimes possible to fix responsibility for repairs upon private individuals or corporate bodies; and it is only by so doing that the pre-1835 liability of parishes can be avoided.

Liability may become fixed upon individuals or corporate bodies (other than local authorities acting as such) in several ways. It sometimes arises out of tenure (*ratione tenuræ*), as when from time immemorial the occupier and his predecessors in title have done repairs to the road in question and there is evidence of some legal origin, such as a grant from the Crown or an admission of legal liability arising out of a grant of land in consideration of repair. The fact, however, that a person has done repairs on his own land or for his own benefit is insufficient to create liability. When liability can be proved, it attaches to the tenure of the land and liability to repair can be enforced in the first place upon the occupier, even though he is not owner. The following are some of the principal recorded decisions in *ratione tenuræ* cases: *R v Blakemore* (1852) 16 JP 147 (immemorial usage); *Daventry Rural District Council v Parker* [1900] 1 QB 1 (enforceable only against the occupier, not against an owner not in occupation); *Ferrand v Bingley Urban District Council* [1903] 2 KB 445; *Esher etc Urban District Council v Marks* (1902) 66 JP 243 (as to origin of liability); *R v Bamber* (1843) 5 QB 279; and *R v Pickering (Township)* (1877) 41 JP 564.

Another way in which liability may arise against individuals or corporate bodies originates in enclosure (*ratione clausuræ*). It is almost impossible that a new case of liability should arise under this heading at the present day, but it arose when a roadway passed over unenclosed land and the public acquired a right to deviate at times when the roadway was impassable. Then, if the adjoining owner enclosed his land by a fence so as to prevent this, he became liable to keep that part of the highway in repair from which the public had the right to deviate. In *Dunscomb's Case* (1634) Cro Car 366, the simple rule was laid down that the owner of the land over which there is an open roadway may fence in his land; but he must leave a sufficient roadway and keep it repaired at his own charge. Another case in which this aspect was discussed is *Henn's Case* (1633) W Jo 296, in which a similar rule was laid down; but cf *R v Stoughton* (1670) 2 Saund 157, where the court held that the rule applied only where the public were deprived of the right of deviation. If the enclosure takes place at the present time with the consent of the highway authority, no liability to maintain will rise: Highways Act 1980, s 51.

Again, liability may depend upon some statutory obligation, as in the case of *R v Sheffield Canal Co* (1849) 13 QB 913, where a local Act of Parliament provided that the company should make a good road to a certain place and keep the same in repair. See also *R v Heaven* (1834) 1 LT (os) 552; *Little Bolton (Inhabitants) v R* (1843) 7 JP 638; *R v Wolverhampton (Inhabitants)* (1845) 9 JP 310.

Where a private individual is liable under a special enactment or by reason of tenure, enclosure or prescription to maintain a footpath or bridleway, the Highways Act 1980, s 41(1) does not relieve such individual of his liability: *ibid*, s 50(1).

4 Liability of local authorities

The local highway authority (ie, normally the county council: 1980 Act, s 1(2); the Secretary of State is responsible in the case of trunk and special roads) are responsible for the repair of all highways maintainable at the public expense which are vested in them (Highways Act 1980, ss 36, 41). These include (*ibid*, s 36(2)) highways constructed by the authority or its predecessors, 'ancient' roads (ie those that were highways prior to 1836: Act of 1835, s 23), roads that have been adopted since 1835, public paths, former 'roads used as public paths' (1981 Act, s 54(4)), and certain footpaths at the side of roads (*Robinson v Richmond (Surrey) Borough Council*, above). In addition, when a public path comes into existence in consequence of a 'public path creation agreement' or the making of a 'public path creation order,' the local highway authority are required to survey the path and carry out such work of making up as may be certified by them to be necessary: 1980 Act, s 27.

Further, whether or not the formalities of s 23 of the 1835 Act have been complied with, it may be presumed that, where a highway authority have in the past themselves carried out repairs in a highway, they regarded that highway as maintainable at the public expense (see eg *Att-Gen v Watford Rural District Council* [1912] 1 Ch 417; *Cababé v Walton-on-Thames Urban District Council* [1914] AC 102). Nevertheless, such a presumption cannot lightly be raised, and the mere fact that the authority have carried out some repairs under emergency powers or in unusual conditions is not of itself sufficient to establish that the authority considered themselves liable to repair the highway (see *Alsager Urban District Council v Barratt* [1965] 2 QB 343).

Parish or community councils may, under s 30 of the Act of 1980 (and compare s 50, *ibid*, p 51), assume responsibility for the maintenance and repair of a particular highway (including a footpath) in the parish which has been dedicated pursuant to an agreement with them. It is, however, no duty of the parish council to provide direction posts, although they may agree to maintain gates or stiles. Where the parish council have resolved to take action under this section, the way will be a highway, but not one maintainable at the public expense and so not the responsibility of the county council as highway authority.

Alternatively, a parish or community council may undertake the maintenance of any footpath or bridleway in the parish which is a highway maintainable at the public expense, under s 43(1) of the 1980 Act.

When any question arises, therefore, as to the repair of footpaths, stiles or small footbridges, it should first be ascertained, outside urban areas, whether the parish council have implemented the above section; if not, recourse should normally be had direct to the county council (see p 56).

5 Enforcement

Proceedings for enforcement of a duty to maintain a highway are now much simpler than they were before the passing of the 1959 Act; for details, see p 56 et seq and p 84 et seq.

6 Termination of liability

The liability of individuals and corporate bodies to repair public roadways, when it actually exists, may be terminated by agreement with the local authority under the Highways Act 1980, s 38, which empowers a local highway authority to enter into an agreement with any person liable to maintain a highway to take upon themselves its maintenance upon terms to be arranged (see model agreement under the Highways Act 1980 s 38 at Appendix 1). Such an agreement effectively discharges the liability *ratione tenuræ* of an owner (*Re Earl of Stamford and Warrington* [1911] 1 Ch 648). However, such an agreement may create an overriding interest within s 70 (1)(*a*) of the Land Registration Act 1925, regarding the public right of way see *Overseas Investment Services Ltd v Simcobuild Construction and Another* (1993) *The Times*, 2 November.

Where a roadway has been destroyed, as by encroachment of the sea (*R v Bamber* (1843) 5 QB 279), or by conversion into a macadamised road (*R v Barker* (1890) 25 QB 213), or materially altered by being declared a main road (*Health v Weaverham Township Overseers* [1894] 2 QB 108), or replaced by a new road (*R v Surgashall* (1854) 23 LT (os) 78), the liability to repair fixed upon a private individual or corporate body comes to an end. But where highways are merely widened by the local authority under statutory powers and not materially altered in character, persons or bodies liable to repair (*ratione tenuræ* or otherwise) will remain liable to contribute their proportionate share towards repair, and the provisions of the 1980 Act relating to public paths do not affect any existing private liabilities, *ratione tenuræ* or otherwise, to maintain a public path (1980 Act, s 50(1)).

7 Meaning of 'maintenance'

What is covered by the word 'maintain' and to what extent repairs to a roadway or footpath can be enforced, are matters of considerable importance. Generally, it may be said that a public roadway must be kept in such repair as to be safe and usable by the ordinary traffic of the district, but the courts will not enter into details. The whole position of local authorities in the matter was discussed by the House of Lords in *Sharpness New Docks v Att-Gen* [1915] AC 654, which was approved in *LNER v North Riding County Council* [1936] AC 365, but these cases must now be read in the light of the Highways (Miscellaneous Provisions) Act 1961 (since replaced by the Highways Act 1980, see p 84).

In *Henry Butt & Co Ltd v Weston-super-Mare Urban District Council* [1922] 1 AC 340, it was held to be the duty of a highway authority to maintain any particular highway in a condition to carry the ordinary traffic on that highway in whatever form the ordinary traffic might develop. That means simply that, as traffic increases or changes in character, the local highway authority should act accordingly in properly maintaining the road to meet the changed circumstances.

The older decisions laid down as a general principle that the parish were not bound to keep a footway in better condition than that in which it had normally existed; but in *R v High Halden (Inhabitants)* (1859) 1 F & F 678, it was held by Blackburn J in the case of an old soft clay road which became unusable in winter-time that, although the parish were not bound to make the road hard, they must in some way, by using stone or hard substances, make it reasonably passable. Extensive repairs, amounting to a major improvement, to a footpath would normally require the consent of the owner and occupier of the land over which the path runs: *Radcliffe v Marsden Urban District Council* (1908) 72 JP 475. In *Winch v Thames Conservators* (1872) 36 JP 646, the court held that the defendants, having power to maintain and repair a towpath and having invited the public to use it, were under a duty to keep it in a reasonably fit condition for use. Where a roadway crosses the bed of a river, and water washes over it at every tide, sweeping away materials for repair, the responsible authority will not be required to do futile repairs: *R v Landulph (Inhabitants)* (1834) 1 M & Rob 393.

The duty to maintain a highway put upon a highway authority under s 41 of the 1980 Act includes a duty to repair (1980 Act, s 329(1)), but this does not include a duty to remove artificial obstructions such as wire fences etc. The duty may extend to the clearance of snow and ice from a slippery footpath (although in *Haydon v Kent CC* [1978] QB 343 it was acknowledged that the County Council had a defence in that they had had no reasonable opportunity of acting after a snowfall, at the time of the accident in question. Similarly in *Bartlett v Department of Transport* (1984) 83 LGR 579, the defendants were not found liable as their failure to have the snow removed was not blameworthy). The duty also extends to the clearance of obstructions occasioned by natural causes, such as vegetation growing on a footpath: *Hereford and Worcester CC v Newman* [1975] 1 WLR 901. But, the collection of flood water in a road after heavy rainfall was not of itself evidence of non-repair or lack of maintenance: *Pritchard v Clwyd County Council* (1992) *The Times*, 16 July. The standard of repair required by the duty to maintain is further discussed at p 85.

Proceedings for enforcement of the express duty to maintain a highway may be taken by a private individual (without any need for him to prove that he is a person aggrieved: *Hereford and Worcester CC v Newman*) against the highway authority in respect of highways maintainable at the public expense, under the Highways Act 1980, s 56 or in the case of privately maintainable highways, under s 57, *ibid*. Breach of the duty to repair can give rise to liability on the part of a highway authority to users of the highway for resulting damage, but s 58 of the 1980 Act provides a defence to such proceedings, discussed at p 85 *et seq*.

8 Gates, stiles, etc

The liability to repair gates, stiles, stepping-stones, etc on public ways rested in effect at common law upon the same basis as the liability to repair the surface. If a right of way is dedicated to and accepted by the public, the latter take it subject to the existence of these erections and similar obstructions—even gates which were in existence at the time of dedication: *Att-Gen v Meyrick and Jones* (1915) 79 JP 515. The liability to maintain and repair any stile or other object which actually forms part of the highway rested upon the local authority at common law—assuming the local authority were responsible for surface repairs.

However, under the 1980 Act, s 146 it is now the duty of the 'owner' (see s 329(1)) of the land to maintain in a safe condition and state of repair any 'stile, gate or other similar structure' across a footpath or bridleway; the standard of repair required is such as 'to prevent unreasonable interference with the rights of the persons using the footpath or bridleway'. This duty may be carried out by the highway authority in any case of default; they may after fourteen days' notice to the owner, carry out any necessary steps of repair and recover not more than three-quarters of the expenses reasonably incurred thereby, from the owner of the land (see also below). This section will not apply where the authority have agreed in writing to maintain the stile or gate, etc, or where conditions are in force under s 147 (see below). Primarily this statutory duty is enforceable by the highway authority by means of the machinery just described, but it seems that an action for damages would lie for breach of statutory duty at the suit of any member of the public using the way and exercising reasonable care, who is injured as a consequence of the faulty condition of a gate or stile across the way, and the case of *Rundle v Hearle* [1898] 2 QB 83, would now presumably be decided differently.

It is the practice of some highway authorities to provide a 'stile kit' to landowners in appropriate circumstances.

In addition, a parish council may use the powers given to them by s 43 of the Act of 1980, to repair gates and stiles on public footpaths, but they cannot be compelled to do so; and it seems that this power has not been affected by the duty imposed by s 146 above. The parish council probably may remove or repair a gate, or substitute a new gate, without the consent of the owner of the soil, provided they give equal facilities to the public; if they substitute gates for stiles, they should obtain the consent of the landowner. (A decision to this effect was given in 1898 by the then Local Government Board upon a case of surcharge by a district auditor.)

New stiles or gates across a footpath or bridleway may be authorised by the highway authority in the interests of agriculture, under s 147(1) of the Act of 1980, and in such a case the authority will normally impose conditions for maintenance and for enabling the way to be exercised without undue inconvenience to the public.

Cases sometimes arise in which a wall by the side of a highway is out of repair. It may be a wall above or below the actual surface of the highway. Here, again, the question of liability to repair will be settled by applying the general principle as to liability for maintenance of the highway itself; but a preliminary question will arise as to whether the wall forms part of the highway or is upon the private premises of an adjoining owner. Reference to several decided cases on wall subsidences will show the legal position. In *R v Lordsmere (Inhabitants)* (1886) 51 JP 86, it was held that whether a dangerous wall which supports a highway is part of that highway is a question of fact for the jury to decide. In *Stockport etc Highway Board v Grant* (1882) 46 JP 437, where an easement of support by a wall had been acquired by the public for a highway, and there was no express stipulation as to repair, the local authority and not the owner of the wall were held responsible for repairs; and the fact that the owner of the wall and his predecessors had upon several occasions repaired the wall did not justify any inference of liability on their part (*Short v Hammersmith Corporation* (1910) 75 JP 82). If a wall is not part of a highway, its repair is no business of the local authority, but of its owner, who will also be liable for damages if injury is caused to any person (*Gibraltar Sanitary Commissioners v Orfila* (1890) 15 App Cas 400).

9 Direction posts

By the Highway Act 1835, s 24 it was made the duty of the surveyor of every parish (except within three miles of the General Post Office, London), with the consent of the vestry or by the direction of the justices, to erect or fix in the most convenient place where two or more highways meet a stone or post, legibly inscribed with the name of the next market town, village, or other place to which the said highways respectively lead, but this duty has now been abolished.

A highway authority now have a general power, after consultation with owners and occupiers of the land concerned, to erect and maintain signposts (or 'other signs or notices serving the same purpose') along any footpath or bridleway or byway open to all traffic (Countryside Act 1968, s 27(1), (7) as amended by the 1981 Act, s 65), and any other person may erect and maintain such posts with the consent of the highway authority (s 27(5) *ibid*). The authority are under an express duty to erect and maintain a signpost at every point where a footpath, bridleway or byway leaves a metalled road except in a case where they are satisfied that such a signpost is not necessary and the parish council (or parish meeting) agree (*ibid*, s 27(2), (3)). This does not give the parish or community council a right of veto to the putting up of a sign; on the contrary, the parish or community council's consent must be obtained if a signpost is considered to be unnecessary. In addition, the highway authority have an unlimited duty to erect such signposts as may in their opinion be required 'to assist persons unfamiliar with the locality to follow the course of a footpath, bridleway or byway' (ibid, s 27(4)). It is clear from subs (7) that 'signposts' in the section includes waymarks, and the Countryside Commission have recommended the use of a standard form of waymark (See their pamphlet 'Waymarking for Public Rights of Way).

The erection on or near any public paths of a false or misleading notice such as is likely to deter the public from using the way is made an offence under the National Parks and Access to the Countryside Act 1949, s 57, and it is the duty of the highway authority to enforce the provisions of that section. Further, the pulling down or obliteration of a traffic sign, milestone or direction post is made an offence by the Highways Act 1980, s 131(2) and the Countryside Act 1968, s 27(6). The latter subsection confers powers of entry on privately owned land for the purposes of erecting a signpost. It is the view of the Countryside Commission that the powers of the highway authority to erect signposts must include a power to erect the post in the soil of the right of way.

10 Wardens

It has for some time been lawful for a local authority to appoint wardens for National and Country Parks. Now under s 62 of the 1981 Act, a local authority (presumably this includes not only a county council but also a district council) may appoint such number of wardens as they may consider necessary or expedient as respects a footpath, bridleway or byway open to all traffic which is both in the 'countryside' (a term which is not defined) and within their area. The purpose for which such wardens may be appointed is 'to advise and assist the public in connection with the use of the path or way'.

11 Field paths: ploughing up

It often happens that footpaths have no strictly defined line—for instance, across a field. What in such a case are the rights of the public? The common law is clear that, if it can be shown that a footway across a field was originally granted to the public subject to a right of ploughing up from time to time, the public cannot complain when it is ploughed up. Similarly, if it can be shown that it has in fact been ploughed up from time to time that amounts to the same thing, and no complaint could be made of 'damaging' the highway contrary to the Highways Act 1980, s 131 (see, eg *Mercer v Woodgate* (1870) LR 5 QB 26 (decided on a similar provision in the Highway Act 1835, s 72)). But if the field has existed for a long period as a grass field and has never during that period been ploughed up, then it might be difficult to justify ploughing.

In *Dennis & Sons Ltd v Good* (1918) 83 JP 110, a grass field crossed by footpaths had been ploughed up and planted with potatoes compulsorily under the Defence of the Realm Regulations. The appellants were convicted under the Highway Act 1835, s 72 of wilfully destroying or injuring the surface of a highway, the highway in question being the footpaths. The Divisional Court upheld this conviction on the ground that the regulations under which the appellants were required to do ploughing did not authorise the War Agricultural Executive Committee to order ploughing up of public footpaths.

It follows from the decision that a footpath across a grass field must be maintained in the event of the remainder of the field being converted into arable land, subject to the legislation discussed below. In *Harrison v Danby* (1870) 34 JP 759, the occupier of land over which a public footpath existed ploughed it up. On information against him under the Highway Act 1835, s 72 it was proved that the field was once a grass common, and about 30 years before had been enclosed and cultivated as arable land. No witness remembered whether it had been ploughed up till 13 years before the case; since that date it had occasionally been ploughed up. It was held that the justices were right in presuming that the road had not been dedicated subject to the occupier ploughing it up and that they had rightly convicted the occupier.

In *Arnold v Blaker* (1871) LR 6 QB 433, the inhabitants had a right of footpath across the plaintiff's field, which from time immemorial had regularly been ploughed up. The local surveyor 'repaired' the pathway so effectively that the plaintiff could not plough it up, and it was held that the surveyor was a trespasser. In *Radcliffe v Marsden Urban District Council* (1908) 72 JP 475, it was held that the local surveyor had no right under guise of repairing a public footway to 'improve' it into a more commodious pathway than it was before: nor to build a footbridge where no such means of crossing a stream existed before. In *Sutcliffe v Sowerby Highways Surveyor* (1859) 23 JP 758 where a footway across a brook had stepping-stones which the defendants removed and replaced by flagstones forming an effective crossing place, it was also held that this was a trespass, and that the landowners were entitled to remove the flagstones without being liable for obstruction under the Highway Act 1835, s 72.

Without prejudice to any such ancient rights of ploughing that it may be possible to establish in a particular case, s 134 of the 1980 Act provided a statutory right to plough up a right of way in the interests of good husbandry, subject to an obligation to make good the route's surface within two weeks. From the perspective of farmers this power was too limited, as it only provided a right to engage in ploughing and not other mechanical processes (eg harvesting) which might temporarily affect the surface of a path or bridleway. Consequently, many farmers ignored these statutory provisions.

In an attempt to achieve a fairer balance between the users of paths and farmers, the Ministry of Agriculture in 1986 sent all farmers a voluntary code of practice on 'Ploughing and Rights of Way'. But, a great number of farmers continued to interfere with the public's use of rights of way (a survey undertaken by the Countryside Commission in 1988 disclosed that a walker or rider had only a 70 per cent chance of travelling two miles along unmetalled public rights of way without encountering difficulties, the most common of which were the ploughing up of routes and the coverage of these routes by growing crops). Therefore, the Environment minister referred the matter to the Official Rights of Way Committee which convened a working party to review changes in the legislation. Representatives of relevant interest groups (including the National Farmers Union and the Ramblers' Association) participated in the ensuing deliberations. The subsequent report was taken up by Mr Edward Leigh MP as a private member's Bill and enacted as the Rights of Way Act 1990.

The new Act seeks to secure a better balance between the interests of farmers and users of rights of way by both extending the rights of farmers and creating new criminal penalties for disturbing the surface of footpaths and bridleways. First, the 1990 Act adds a new section to the Highways Act 1980 (s 131A), which makes it an offence for a person, without lawful authority or excuse, to disturb the surface of a footpath, bridleway or other highway not comprising a made-up carriageway, so as to render it inconvenient for the exercise of the public right of way. Interestingly, only highway authorities, district, parish and community councils are authorised to initiate prosecutions for this offence—presumably to prevent vexatious proceedings by over-zealous private persons or organisations.

Secondly, s 134 of the Highways Act 1980 is repealed and replaced by a new wider power enabling the occupier of agricultural land to 'plough or otherwise disturb the surface' of a footpath or bridleway which passes over a field, when acting in accordance with the rules of good husbandry. However, the farmer must make good the surface of the right of way (to not less than its minimum width: defined in a new Schedule 12A of the Highways Act 1980 as being 1 metre for footpaths crossing fields and 2 metres for bridleways crossing fields) and indicate the line of the right of way on the ground within 14 days of disturbing the route (note the highway authority can extend this period by a further 28 days). This power does not apply to excavations or engineering operations. If the occupier fails to comply with the restoration duties laid down in the Act, the local highway authority is provided with two sanctions; either it can either prosecute the occupier for a new offence of not restoring the surface/indicating the line of the right of way, or it can itself undertake the necessary restoration work and recover its costs from the occupier.

Thirdly, the Act entitles occupiers of agricultural land to apply to their local highway authority for an order enabling them to disturb the surface of paths and bridleways for up to three months during which necessary excavation or engineering operations can be undertaken. The authority may impose conditions on the order for the protection and convenience of users of the rights of way. Again, if the occupier fails to make good the surface of the right of way within the specified time period, the highway authority can either prosecute or undertake chargeable restoration work.

Finally, the 1990 Act makes it an offence for an occupier of agricultural land to allow any crop, other than grass (defined as a variety or mixture commonly used for pasture, silage or haymaking), to encroach on a footpath or bridleway so as to render it inconvenient for the exercise of the public right of way. Alleged breaches of this offence can be prosecuted by any individual or organisation (eg a local amenity group). The Act also places an express duty on highway authorities to enforce this provision.

In August 1990 the Department of the Environment issued a circular (17/90) to local authorities on the Rights of Way Act 1990.

The circular stressed that local authorities have a key role in securing the success of the Act's goals and that the authorities have been granted new enforcement powers. But, the government's view was that conciliation, rather than confrontation with farmers, was the preferred course of action.

The Ramblers' Association brought its first prosecution under the 1990 Act in Selby magistrates' court during November 1991. The Association asserted that two landowners had allowed a crop of wheat to encroach upon a footpath which crossed a field and had also failed to indicate the line of the path. The defendant landowners entered a plea of guilty and the magistrates ordered a conditional discharge with the defendants paying £200 towards the Association's costs (*Footpath Worker* Vol 13 No 1 p 11).

A number of successful prosecutions have been brought by several local authorities (including Suffolk County Council, Staffordshire County Council, Humberside County Council and Leicestershire County Council) under the 1990 Act against farmers who have failed to restore rights of way after ploughing and/or who allowed crops to encroach on highways (see *Footpath Worker* Vol 14 No 2 p 17). In the light of a nationwide survey conducted during 1992, the Ramblers' Association has concluded that automatic compliance with the requirements of the 1990 Act by farmers is 'still fairly unusual but there are signs that this will slowly improve, particularly as the number of prosecutions increases' (*Footpath Worker*, Vol 13 No 4 p 16).

12 Repair of bridges

The burden of repairing bridges in public highways lies on the highways authority because a bridge is part of the highway: 1980 Act, s 328(2). But a bridge will now become a publicly maintained bridge only if it is constructed by the highway authority, or adopted by them, or if they agree to undertake its maintenance under s 38 of the 1980 Act (as amended by the New Roads and Street Works Act 1991, s 22; also see model agreement at Appendix 1, and p 11).

In *Re Staffordshire and Derbyshire County Councils* (1890) 54 JP 566, a bridge at Burton-on-Trent stood partly within each of two counties. By a local Act it was provided that the respective county rates should share the cost of maintenance. Under the provisions of the Local Government Act 1888, s 50, Burton became wholly included in the County of Stafford. It was held that, notwithstanding this, the local Act remained in force and both counties were still liable to pay equally for repair. If such a case arose today, responsibility for the bridge and approaches thereto is determined, in the event of disagreement, as between the two highway authorities by the Secretary of State: Highways Act 1980, s 3.

The local authority may not place a footbridge over a stream where no bridge already exists, by way of making it more commodious for the public (see *Radcliffe v Marsden UDC*, p 60 above). If a private person erects a bridge on a roadway over which the public have or acquire a right of passage, the liability to repair it falls upon the highway authority (*R v Southampton County* (1887) 19 QBD 590). Bridges built prior to the passing of the Bridges Act 1803 are repairable by the highway authority unless there are particular circumstances fixing liability upon some other person (see *Att-Gen v West Riding etc* (1903) 67 JP 173). Where a railway company (now the British Railways Board) has been placed under a statutory obligation to construct a bridge and to form a roadway thereover, it will be under a duty to maintain not only the bridge itself, but also the roadway over the bridge and the approaches on either side: *LNER v North Riding County Council* [1936] AC 365. (As to the extent of liability for the 'immediate approaches', see *Monmouthshire County Council v British Transport Commission* [1957] 1 WLR 1146. As to bridges generally, see p 11.)

Chapter 5

The Protection of Public Rights of Way

In Chapter 1 we established that the grant of a right of way is merely a right of passing and re-passing (whether it be of footway, bridleway, carriageway or otherwise) and that the public acquire by dedication no right of property in the soil. We may now inquire more precisely as to the relations which exist, after dedication, between the owner of the soil and the authorities charged with the administration of highway law.

1 Rights of owner of soil

The owner of the soil, after dedication, retains all his rights in the soil and may exercise those rights just as he pleases, so long as he does not interfere with the public right of passing and re-passing along the surface. This, however, is subject to certain statutory modifications. (see eg. p 59) Apart from these, the general legal presumption is that the ownership of the soil of a highway remains vested in the adjoining owners on either side of the centre of the way (*ad medium filum*): so that where the same person is owner of the land on both sides, the entire way belongs to him (subject to the surface rights of the public). We have already seen that the right to navigate a river is a right of highway; which gives rise to the same legal presumption of ownership by the proprietors on either bank to the line of mid-stream.

Where a highway is maintainable at the public expense, the 'top crust' of the highway surface (be it road or footpath) vests in the highway authority, so far as is sufficient to enable the public to exercise their rights to pass and repass and to permit services to be laid under the surface by public utility undertakings (subject to compliance with the New Roads and Street Works Act 1991, Part

III). For some purposes, eg liability to payment of tithe redemption annuity, this is sufficient to constitute the highway authority owners of the highway: *Tithe Redemption Commission v Runcorn Urban District Council* [1954] Ch 383. Furthermore, it enables the highway authority to invoke the summary procedure (under RSC Ord 113) for the removal of trespassers on the highway: *Wiltshire County Council v Frazer* (1984) 47 P & CR 69. However, the highway authority have vested in them only sufficient air space above the highway to enable the highway to be used by traffic and for telephone wires etc, and other objects lawfully erected in the highway: *New Towns Commission v Hemel Hempstead Corporation* [1962] 1 WLR 1158.

The retained ownership of the subsoil may carry with it very important advantages—especially in rural districts, as will be seen from the following:

In *R v Pratt* (1855) 4 El & Bl 860, the defendant was convicted under the Game Act 1831 of trespassing in pursuit of game on 'land in the possession and occupation of' the prosecutor, who, as the lord of the manor, owned the land on both sides of the highway. The defence was that he was on the highway; but the court held that that made no difference, seeing that the soil of the highway belonged to the prosecutor, and that the defendant was upon the highway not for the lawful purpose of passing and repassing, but for the unlawful purpose of pursuing game. His conviction by the magistrates was therefore upheld.

In *Harrison v Duke of Rutland* [1893] 1 QB 142, the duke's grouse-moor was crossed by a public pathway, and the plaintiff went upon this way for the purpose of interfering with the duke and his guests by preventing the driving of grouse towards the butts. Having been forcibly removed by the duke's keepers, he brought an action for damages; but the court held that he was a trespasser and that the forcible removal was justifiable in the circumstances.

In *Hickman v Maisey* [1900] 1 QB 752, the defendant, who was employed by a 'sporting' journal, insisted upon loitering about the highway adjoining the plaintiff's land for the purpose of watching racehorses being exercised and of taking notes about them. An action of trespass resulted in a verdict for the plaintiff from which the defendant unsuccessfully appealed. In the Court of Appeal it was held that the defendant had exceeded the ordinary and reasonable user of the highway to which, as a member of the public, he was entitled. See also *Randall v Tarrant* [1955] 1 WLR 255 where it was suggested that the owner of a motor vehicle parked on the highway for an unreasonable time or an unlawful purpose may be guilty of trespass.

The owner may be entitled to plough up a footpath if the path was dedicated subject to such a right (see p 59) or he may plough up the path by following the procedure of the Rights of Way Act 1990 (ibid).

2 Roadside strips and waste

It is also convenient to consider the frequently recurring question as to what is the width of a highway. This issue may arise with any highway—an ordinary high road with a metalled part and footpaths or grass verges on one or both sides, or a mere footpath through fields or woodlands. In every case the actual width of the roadway over which the public have a right to pass and re-pass is a question of fact. Bearing in mind the presumption that the right of passage was originally dedicated to the public and that the subsoil of the way therefore remains in the owner or owners, it is often a matter of serious importance to determine what (if any) particular width was dedicated. There will not normally be any right to deviate if the way has become founderous (see p 22); if the way is obstructed (eg by a fallen tree), the obstruction can be removed by a member of the public.

One of the most frequent occasions upon which this question arises is in regard to waste land (generally grass verges) by the side of country roads; and the issue is whether the highway extends from hedge to hedge or whether it is limited to the metalled part over which vehicles and foot-passengers alike pass along. In some cases— eg where an Inclosure Act has laid down the precise width—the matter raises no difficulty. In the case of a public path duly recorded in the course of a survey made under the National Parks and Access to the Countryside Act 1949, Pt IV or the Act of 1981, the written statement may (and should) define the width of the path, and this will constitute conclusive evidence (1981 Act, s 56(1)(e) and p 31). In other cases the question of width resolves itself into a pure question of evidence. Aerial photographs may well be a valuable source of such evidence provided they are accurately dated. Numerous cases have been decided upon the subject, a perusal of which will show not only the general legal principles acted upon by the courts but also the type of evidence accepted.

The general presumption that the highway extends between the outer edge of hedges (see *Turner v Ringwood Highway Board* (1870) LR 9 Eq 418) until the contrary be shown, was applied in such cases as *Harvey v Truro Rural District Council* [1903] 2 Ch 638. (See also an article by the present author at 101 SJ 218). However, in *Att-Gen v Beynon* [1970] Ch 1, it was said that the mere fact that a road runs between fences or hedges does not of itself give rise to a presumption that the way extends between the fences. A preliminary question must first be answered, namely, whether the fences (or hedges) were erected by reference to the highway so as to separate the adjoining closes therefrom. Only when that question has been affirmatively answered does a rebuttable presumption of law arise to the effect that the way extends between the fences or hedges. The preliminary question is, however, said Goff J in this case, to be decided 'in the sense that the fences do mark the limit of the highway unless there is something in the condition of the road or the circumstances to the contrary' (at p 268).

If there is a ditch at the side of the verge, and this was not constructed by the highway authority, it will be presumed *not* to be part of the highway (*Hanscombe v Bedfordshire County Council* [1938] Ch 944). See also *Att-Gen and Croydon Rural District Council v Moorsom-Roberts* (1908) 72 JP 123; *Offin v Rochford Rural District Council* [1906] 1 Ch 342; *Hinds and Diplock v Breconshire County Council* [1938] 4 All ER 24; and *Countess of Belmore v Kent County Council* [1901] 1 Ch 873, in which it was pointed out that acts of ownership, such as grazing cattle, may be sufficient to rebut the presumption of dedication in respect of a roadside verge. Trees and shrubs must not generally be planted within 15 ft from the centre of a made-up carriageway, unless a licence has been obtained from the local highway authority (Highways Act 1980, ss 141 and 142).

In the case of a footpath across open land or through woodlands, the way must be wide enough to allow for passage in single file, but if a greater width is claimed, evidence of actual user would have to be adduced.

3 Highway authorities and their responsibilities

County councils, London borough councils, metropolitan district councils, district councils, and parish and, in Wales, community councils to a less extent, are all concerned with highways. The Secretary of State also exercises authority—partly as 'supervisory' authority in regard to highway matters arising under the Public

Health, Housing, and Town and Country Planning and other Acts (in this case it will be the Secretary of State for the Environment), and partly as highway authority in his own right under the Road Traffic and the Highways Acts (but in this case it will be the Secretary of State for Transport).

The former law was consolidated in the Highways Act 1959, subsequently replaced by the Highways Act 1980, and highway administration was substantially changed by the Local Government Act 1972. Under this statute, apart from trunk and special roads, the county council are the highway authority for all their area. This distribution of functions has now been affected by the abolition of the Greater London Council and the other metropolitan county councils: the Local Government Act 1985.

The district councils are not highway authorities in their own right, but under the 1972 Act, s 187 they *may* undertake the maintenance within their area of such footpaths, bridleways and urban roads (not being trunk roads or classified roads) as are highways maintainable at the public expense. The district councils also have a few other highway functions, as will appear. All roadways thus taken over by the county councils are repairable by the county council if, when taken over, they were maintainable at the public expense (see p 48); but certain trunk roads and special roads have been transferred to the Department of Transport as highway authority, and by s 50(1) of the 1980 Act the existing liability of any person or body of persons to maintain and repair any highway has been preserved. In London, the London borough councils and the Common Council of the City are the highway authority for all highways (except trunk roads): 1980 Act, s 1(3) as amended by the Local Government Act 1985, s 8. The term 'highway' is defined in the Highway Act 1835 (s 5), as meaning 'all roads, bridges (not being county bridges), carriageways, cartways, horseways, bridleways, footways, causeways, churchways and pavements', but there is no real definition at all of the word in the 1980 Act (see s 328); and see p 2.

Highway authorities may delegate certain of their functions by way of agency agreements. Whilst statutory duties remain with the highway authority, in practice it can be important to establish which council is responsible for carrying out functions and the respective rights and liabilities set out in the Agency Agreement.

Note: Currently the Local Government Commission are reviewing the structures for local government in different parts of England

and their recommendations may well result in changes to the allocation of responsibility for highways.

4 The defence of public rights

The duties and powers of local authorities in regard to the protection of public rights contained in the Highways Act 1959 were varied by the Local Government Act 1972. These provisions have now been replaced by the 1980 Act, the substantive provision being s 130 of that Act.

In the first place it is made the express duty of every highway authority (ie the Secretary of State, the county council or the metropolitan district council) 'to assert and protect the rights of the public to the use and enjoyment of any highway for which they are the highway authority' (s 130(1)). The highway authority also have a duty to prevent any unlawful encroachment on any roadside waste comprised in a highway for which they are the highway authority (s 130(4)), and it is their duty to prevent, so far as possible, the stopping up or obstruction of such highways (s 130(3)). Finally, by s 130(2), the county council, a London borough council, the Common Council of the City of London or a district council may assert and protect the rights of the public to the use and enjoyment of any highway or roadside waste in their area, in respect of which they are not the highway authority.

The effect of this duty 'to assert and protect the rights of the public' was considered in *R v Lancashire CC, ex p Guyer* [1980] 1 WLR 1024. The Court of Appeal held that the section did not require a highway authority to commence legal proceedings claiming the existence of a right of way in circumstances where they had no faith in the claims made by members of the public. There was a serious dispute concerning the status of the footpath in question and therefore the authority could not be compelled by *mandamus* to take action under the section.

A county council must take appropriate action under this section if a parish or (in Wales) a community council make representations to them under s 130(6). This does not mean that the county council are obliged to act precisely as asked by the parish council, but they must exercise their discretion properly, taking all relevant considerations into account, in particular the rights of the public entitled to use the way in question (see *R v Surrey County Council; ex p Send Parish Council* [1979] JPL 613). Subsection (5) gives a highway authority or other council the power to institute or defend legal proceedings and generally to take such steps as they deem expedient to give effect to those duties or powers.

Section 137 of the 1980 Act creates an offence of wilfully obstructing a highway without lawful authority or excuse. Highway authorities are regularly requested to prosecute for obstruction, particularly of footpaths and bridleways. The threat of prosecution can add the necessary sanction to an authority's request to a person responsible for an obstruction of a highway to clear the way. This provision is considered further at page 91.

As mentioned on p 56, s 56 of the 1980 Act enables any person to take proceedings before the local magistrates for an order requiring a highway authority to perform their duty (under s 41, *ibid*) to keep a highway maintainable at public expense in repair. (There are no restrictions on who may institute proceedings under s 56; as to the sections to which such restrictions apply, see the 1980 Act, s 312 and Sched 22 together with the Local Government (Miscellaneous Provisions) Act 1982, s 21.) In *Hereford and Worcester CC v Newman* [1975] 1 WLR 901, it was held by the Court of Appeal that this section could be used by a member of the public to require the clearance of obstructions on a footpath where it could be established that such clearance was a matter of maintenance of the path.

So wide are these functions given to local authorities (and they replace similar ones given to the old authorities) of dealing with these matters that Neville J in *Holloway v Egham Urban District Council* (1908) 72 JP 433, gave a warning against over-enthusiasm. In that case, adjoining landowners took action against the local authority and asked for a declaration that a certain lane was not a public footway. They succeeded, and an injunction was granted restraining the local authority from trespassing and ordering them to pay the costs. The result was similar in *Thornhill v Weeks (No 2)* [1913] 2 Ch 464, *Thornhill v Weeks (No 3)* [1915] 1 Ch 106, and *Fuller v Chippenham Rural District Council* (1914) 79 JP 4.

An alternative non-judicial method by which an aggrieved individual may seek redress against a highway authority's actions (or inaction) is to make a complaint to the Local Ombudsman under the Local Government Act 1974 (as amended by the Local Government Act 1988 and the Local Government and Housing Act 1989). If the Local Ombudsman finds that a complainant has suffered injustice as a consequence of maladministration by the highway authority he may publish such a finding and the authority are obliged to have regard to the report, but they cannot be compelled in law to implement the Local Ombudsman's recommendations to alleviate the injustice. An example of a successful complaint made by the secretary of the Ramblers' Association in North Wales was issued by the Local Ombudsman in February 1993 (Ref CN: 91/589 published in *Footpath Worker*, Vol 14 No 2 p 4). The complainant alleged that Clwyd County Council had failed to comply with its statutory duty to protect a specified public footpath from obstruction, thereby depriving walkers of their enjoyment in following the path. The definitive map showed the path crossing a farmyard and no objections had been made against that route when the map was created or revised.

However, in 1984 and 1987 a farmer refused to allow members of the public and a council officer to cross the farmyard and, later, he disputed the existence of the right of way across the farmyard. Officers of the authority disagreed as to the best solution of the dispute between walkers and the farmer; one officer favoured the making of a deletion order whilst another preferred a diversion order. No decisive action was undertaken by 1991, when the complaint was made to the Local Ombudsman. The Ombudsman reported that the authority had first been notified of the obstruction eight years earlier and he would have expected the county council to have relied upon the definitive map and thus assert the rights of way shown on it. Instead, the authority had 'dithered' for a number of years and this amounted to maladministration. The complainant had suffered injustice as a result of this maladministration and, therefore, the Local Ombudsman recommended that Clwyd County Council should pay £250 compensation to the complainant and take immediate action to either remove the obstruction or make the appropriate modification order. Other complaints regarding the conduct of highway authorities can be found in the 1991/92 Annual Report of the Local Government Ombudsmen, pp 37–38.

It is sometimes objected that local authorities, in protecting public rights of way, are not entitled to act in a high-handed fashion by breaking down obstructions and otherwise asserting their rights by physical force, as though they were private individuals; but that where a dispute arises it is their duty to act judicially, and if unable to resolve the dispute to compose the matter to go to the courts and seek a judicial decision. This, however, is not a valid objection. It has been laid down in several cases that councils, in carrying out their duties in the protection of public rights, are in the same position as a private individual engaged in protecting his own property (*Murray v Epsom Local Board* [1897] 1 Ch 35), but if a council employs forcible measures and it is proved afterwards that they were in the wrong, they will be liable to pay damages for trespass (*Reynolds v Presteign Urban District Council* [1896] 1 QB 604).

These powers of local authorities were not affected by the passing of the National Parks and Access to the Countryside Act 1949, but normally the local authority should be content to rely on the survey of rights of way made by the authority under the Act (see p 24). In the course of preparing any modification order altering the definitive map and statement the county council as survey authority must consult with the district and parish or community councils within the area (1981 Act, Sched 15, para 1 as amended by the Local Government Act 1985, Sched 3).

5 Parish and community councils

Parish councils (or, in Wales, community councils: see the Local Government Act 1972, s 179(4)) have a right under s 130(6) of the 1980 Act to intervene in regard to any unlawful stopping up or obstruction of any public right of way within their area. They also have an option to undertake the maintenance of public footpaths within their parish, but not so as to relieve any other authority or person from liability to do so (Highways Act 1980, s 43(1)).

Further, parish or community councils are empowered under s 30 of the 1980 Act to agree to the dedication of a highway over land in the parish, provided such dedication is 'beneficial to the inhabitants of the parish or any part thereof'. In any such case the agreement should clearly lay down who is to be responsible for repairs to avoid any future dispute. A general power to acquire land by agreement or compulsorily is given to a parish or community council by the Local Government Act 1972, ss 124, 125 (see also p 56 as to repair of gates and stiles).

Under the Parish Councils Act 1957, a parish or community council may decide to provide seats and shelters on roads (s 1), and to provide lighting for 'roads and other public places' in the parish (s 3).

In the matter of asserting and defending public rights, parish councils may exercise an important power. It is the duty of county councils, the highway authority under the Highways Act 1980, s 130 (see p 70), to assert and protect all public rights of way, by legal proceedings if necessary. Parish and community councils are not in a position to fight legal battles on behalf of the responsible highway authority; but they can compel that authority to take action where necessary. Their powers are to call the attention of the highway authority to any disturbance of public rights, and by s 130(6) they may make representations to the highway authority to the effect that a highway in the parish has been unlawfully stopped up or obstructed, or that there has been an unlawful encroachment on a roadside waste.

It then becomes the duty of the highway authority to take 'proper proceedings' accordingly; a duty which could be enforced by *mandamus* but not apparently if there is doubt about the status of the way in question (see the *Lancashire* case, p 70 above). However, Barker cautions that in practice the role of parish councils in seeking to protect rights of way may be limited because of factors such as:

(1) limited resources;

(2) the priorities of individual councils; and

(3) in many areas there may be strong links between the council and local landowners. Therefore, '. . . a parish council may not take up the issue of obstructed paths with the expected degree of conviction and efficiency' (F Barker, 'Protect and Assert . . . A Guide to s 130 of the Highways Act 1980' [1991] JPL 3 at p 7).

Chapter 6

The Extinguishment and Diversion of Public Rights of Way

1 Introduction

The common law maxim has been said to be 'once a highway always a highway', as the rights of the public cannot be lost merely by non-user (*Dawes v Hawkins* (1860) 8 CB (NS) 848). Thus, in *Turner v Ringwood Highway Board* (1870) LR 9 Eq 418, a public road originally set out in an inclosure award as being 50 ft wide had for years been used to only half that extent, with the result that both sides were covered with furze bushes and fir trees. The highway board began to clear the furze and cut down the trees, and the owner of the adjoining land brought an action to restrain them. The court held, however, that the public rights still extended over the whole 50 ft of the highway, and they dismissed the action. See also *Pullin v Deffel* (1891) 64 LT 134, and *Harvey v Truro Rural District Council* [1903] 2 Ch 638.

Evidence that a way has not been used for 20 years is not sufficient to extinguish public rights. In relation to a claim for public rights over a river, Holroyd J said: 'If the place in question was ever a public navigable river, I apprehend that its ceasing to be used as such for 20 years, and being, during that time, in a condition which is inconsistent with its being used as a public navigable river, would not extinguish the public rights, if they did exist previously to that time' (*Vooght v Winch* (1819) 2 B & Ald 662, at p 670).

The definitive map prepared under the National Parks and Access to the Countryside Act 1949 and any modification made by the survey authority may, by virtue of the 1981 Act, s 56 (see p 31), overrule the common law principle; but if a way is shown as a footpath on the map, this will not exclude evidence that the public have wider rights (1981 Act, s 56(1)(a)).

2 'Ordinary' means of extinguishing public rights of way

The right of passing along a particular highway can, apart from statute, be extinguished only by the natural destruction of the way itself, eg when it is washed away by the sea (*R v Bamber* (1843) 5 QB 279); but not merely by temporary effacement, eg a landslide (*R v Greenhow* (*Inhabitants*) (1876) 1 QBD 703). Apart from total physical extinction, a right of way can be brought to an end only by due process of law (see *Lee v Patrick* (1864) 28 JP Jo 276). Legal process involves either actual stopping-up or else diversion; and, apart from special statutes considered below, especially the Town and Country Planning Act 1990, s 247 the procedure that may be applied in any case to effect either stopping-up or diversion is now laid down in the Highways Act 1980, s 116 which replaces the former complicated procedure of the Highway Act 1835, ss 84–92.

Under this section, the 'appropriate authority' (normally the highway authority: see s 116(2) as amended by the Local Government Act 1985, Sched 17) may apply to the local magistrates for an order that a highway may be stopped up or diverted, on the ground that it is unnecessary or that it can be diverted so as to make it nearer or more commodious to the public. In the case of a diversion, the written consent of the local planning authority must be produced, and also the written consent of every person having a legal interest (see the Law of Property Act 1925, s 1(1) and (2)) in the land over which the highway is to be diverted. No part of a highway is to be stopped up until the new part to be substituted has been completed to the satisfaction of two or more justices, and a certificate to that effect has been transmitted to the clerk of the court. Any stopping-up or diversion order made under this section may provide for the exclusion of all traffic, or be made subject to the reservation of a footpath or bridleway (s 116(4)).

If the highway so to be stopped up or diverted is not a classified road, notice of the proposal must be given to the council of the district where the highway is situated, and to the council of the parish (if any) in which the highway is situated (or to the chairman of the parish meeting if there is no parish council), or, in Wales, to the council of the community in which the highway is situated (Highways Act 1980, s 116(3)). No application can then be made if within two months notice is given to the effect that the council, parish meeting or community council (as the case may be) have refused to consent to the making of the application.

Any person who wants a highway to be stopped up or diverted may request the highway authority to take action under s 116, and the authority may then agree to do so on the basis that such person shall provide for part or the whole of the costs of the proceedings (*ibid*, s 117). Where an aggrieved person (eg a user of the particular highway in question) successfully objects to an application by a highway authority under s 116, the magistrates have the power (under s 64(1) of the Magistrates' Courts Act 1980) to award costs against the authority in favour of the objector: *Lincolnshire County Council v Brewis* (1992) Crown Office CO/730/91 (reported in *Footpath Worker*, Vol 13 No 4 p 8).

If the highway is to be stopped up, it must be shown to be unnecessary—a question of fact for the justices in the particular case. However, Woolf LJ (as he then was) provided some guidance for the justices on the meaning of this term in *The Ramblers' Association v Kent County Council* [1991] JPL 530. Relevant considerations are:

(1) it is the public for whom the particular highway must be unnecessary;

(2) for what purposes would the highway be unnecessary eg for recreational purposes; and

(3) where an alternative way was to be provided it had to be reasonably suitable for the public using the existing way.

Where the highway is to be diverted, it must be shown that the proposed new highway is 'nearer or more commodious to the public'. It is not essential to prove that the diverted way would be nearer *and* more commodious; the magistrates may make an order under either heading. In this context the term commodious was considered by Woolf J (as he then was) to involve the elements of 'convenience', 'utility' and 'spaciousness' (*Gravesham BC v Wilson and Straight* [1983] JPL 607). Any new way which is provided as a diversion of a highway which is maintainable at the public expense will itself be so maintainable provided the new way is constructed by the highway authority, as will normally be the case (1980 Act, s 36(2)(a)). If an existing maintainable way is diverted and the diversion is constructed by or at the expense of a private landowner (perhaps under s 117 of the 1980 Act) it seems that the diversion, being the original way in a different location, should also be maintainable at the public expense, but this case is not expressly provided for in s 36.

The consent of the local authority must be obtained for the lowering of the surface of a public highway for mining or quarrying purposes; see *Hoddesdon Urban District Council v Broxbourne Sand & Ballast Pits Ltd* [1936] 2 KB 19.

3 Special statutory procedures

The Secretary of State for Transport may, by order made under the Town and Country Planning Act 1990 s 247, authorise the stopping up or diversion of any highway where he is satisfied that it is necessary to do so in order to enable development to be carried out in accordance with planning permission granted under Pt III of the 1990 Act. In *Vasiliou v Secretary of State for Transport* [1991] 2 All ER 77, the Court of Appeal held that the Secretary of State was entitled, and should, take account of the directly adverse effect his order would have on all those persons currently entitled to the rights, which would be extinguished if he made an order under s 247, when exercising his discretion. The Court of Appeal quashed the Transport Secretary's order because he had failed to take account of the effect of the order on the trade of a local restaurateur, whose business adjoined the relevant highway. In some cases such an order may be made even when planning permission has not been granted (1990 Act, s 253). A diversion order may be made under s 247 even after the development authorised by the planning permission has been commenced, but not (apparently) once that development has been completed, because of the words 'to be carried out', in the section (see *Ashby v Secretary of State for the Environment* [1980] 1 WLR 679). In practice this provision is the most frequently relied upon to divert highways. There is no power or authority for any person affected by such a diversion to claim compensation.

Further, a local planning authority (sometimes in consultation with the highway authority (see Local Government Act 1972, Sched 16, para 41) may ask the Secretary of Transport to make an order converting a highway into a footpath or bridleway (Town and Country Planning Act 1990, s 249), and in such a case the authority may expend money in providing amenities for pedestrians (Local Government (Miscellaneous Provisions) Act 1982, Sched 5).

By following a procedure similar to s 247 of the 1990 Act, a local planning authority may by order authorise the stopping up or diversion of a footpath or bridleway, but an opportunity has to be given for objections or representations to be made to the Secretary of State for the Environment, who will then normally hold an inquiry (Town and Country Planning Act 1990, ss 257 and 259 and

Sched 14). Forms to be used under this procedure are specified in the Town and Country Planning (Public Path Orders) Regulations 1993 (SI No 10).

The Acquisition of Land Act 1981 (which regulates the procedure for the compulsory acquisition of land by public authorities) provides by s 32 for the extinguishment by order of the Secretary of State for the Environment of public rights of way over land so acquired or which could have been so acquired in default of agreement. A modified version of this procedure may also be used on the application of British Coal for the suspension of a public right of way, under the Housing and Planning Act 1986, Sched 8, para 6.

Special provision is made for the extinction of rights of way over land acquired for slum clearance by the Housing Act 1985, s 294 (and note the Housing (Prescribed Forms) Regulations 1990 (SI No 447)) and similarly in respect of land acquired or appropriated for planning purposes by the Town and Country Planning Act 1990, s 251.

Ways set out under the Inclosure Acts are subject to the provisions of the Inclosure (Consolidation) Act 1801. The Military Manoeuvres Acts 1897 and 1911, as amended by the Land Powers (Defence) Act 1958, Sched 1, contain powers to interfere temporarily with highways; whilst the Military Lands Act 1892 provides for the closing of rural footways near to land in occupation of the military authorities—subject to agreement with the district council. Extinguishment powers also exist under the Defence Act 1842 (this Act was used in July 1990 by the Secretary of State for Defence to stop up a bridleway crossing part of RAF Upper Heyford, in Oxfordshire, on the grounds that nearby stores of aviation fuel presented a danger to users of the highway); but the extinguishment of a private right of way does not necessarily also extinguish public rights over the same soil: *Shonleigh Nominees v Att-Gen* [1974] 1 WLR 305.

Similar powers may be employed where land is, or is to be, used by a government department for the purposes of an installation provided or to be provided for defence purposes; or is used by a manufacturer of aircraft as an airfield wholly or mainly in connection with the manufacture of aircraft for defence purposes (Land Powers (Defence) Act 1958, s 8). Power to extinguish rights of way over land compulsorily purchased is also frequently reserved in private Acts, eg Acts for the promotion of water and other public undertakings; and see the New Towns Act 1981, ss 16 and 23 (as amended by the Telecommunications Act 1984, Sched 4).

There are also special powers to stop up a private access to premises from a highway, either compulsorily or by agreement, under the Highways Act 1980, ss 124–128.

Whether the extinguished right of way be public or private, compensation may be payable, where a claim can be properly established, under the procedure of the Land Compensation Act 1961, in accordance with any specific variations of the procedure of that Act embodied in the particular statute under which the local authority are acting. The right to compensation for injurious affection, though affecting a private individual, may arise out of a public right, eg a right of access to premises by a public highway. If the injury suffered would have given rise to an action for damages at common law, the right to compensation will arise unless specifically excluded by the Act or by any scheme made thereunder. See *Metropolitan Board of Works v McCarthy* (1874) LR 7 HL 243, and *Reckett v Midland Railway Co* (1867) LR 3 CP 82. These principles will apply to cases under the Public Health Act where temporary obstruction of the access may be authorised by the statute, but a general right to compensation in such a case is given by the Public Health Act 1936, s 278; see, eg *Lingke v Christchurch Corporation* [1912] 3 KB 595.

The Highways Act 1980, s 14 gives power to the Secretary of State to make orders authorising the stopping up of highways that cross or enter trunk or classified roads and similar orders may be made in respect of special roads under s 18(1)(c), ibid.

Under the Requisitioned Land and War Works Act 1945, the Secretary of State is empowered to make orders for the permanent stopping up or diversion of highways temporarily stopped up or diverted in the exercise of emergency powers (s 15, as amended by the Requisitioned Land and War Works Act 1948, s 3) and any such order may subsequently be varied or revoked (Land Powers (Defence) Act 1958, s 9).

Other statutes which give powers to divert or extinguish public rights of way for specific purposes include the Water Industry Act 1991, s 167 (for the purpose of works undertaken by water companies) and the Transport and Works Act 1992, Sched 2 (for the construction or operation of railways, tramways, trolley vehicle systems and inland waterways).

The normal procedure for the diversion of a public path (a footpath or bridleway) is by order made by the council within whose area the path is situate (ie the county council or the Metropolitan district council or the London borough council (s 329)), in any case where it appears to them that, in the interests of the owner, lessee or occupier of land crossed by the path, it is expedient that the line of the path or way or part of it should be diverted (Highways Act 1980, s 119 as amended by the 1981 Act, Sched 16, para 5). However, this power cannot be used to extinguish a public path merely by transferring the right of way to another existing path: *Lake District Special Planning Board, ex p Bernstein* (1982) *The Times*, 3 February. Similarly, the council may order a public path to be extinguished on the ground 'that it is not needed for public use' whether or not the owner or occupier etc has asked for such an order to be made (*ibid*, s 118). In both these cases, the consent of the local planning authority has to be obtained (where appropriate; and in a National Park, there must be consultation with the Countryside Commission (s 120)). If the order is opposed it will not be effective until it has been confirmed by the Secretary of State; the procedure of Sched 6 to the 1980 Act, as amended by Sched 16 to the 1981 Act, and of the Public Path Orders Regulations 1993 (SI No 11) will have to be observed and the Secretary of State must have regard to the interests of agriculture and forestry (1980 Act, s 29, applied by s 121(3), *ibid*).

The matters to be considered by the local authority when considering whether to make a stopping-up order are different from those to be evaluated by the Secretary of State when deciding if the order should be confirmed according to the High Court ruling in *R v Secretary of State for the Environment, ex p Cheshire County Council* [1991] JPL 537. Auld J held that the criterion for an authority making an order under the 1980 Act, s 118(1) was whether the footpath was needed for public use. Whereas, the Secretary's duty

was to consider the broader and discretionary question under s 118(2) as to the expediency of making such an order having regard to the extent, if any, to which it appeared to him that the paths would, apart from the order, be likely to be used by the public (at p 539).

As a general rule in these cases of diversions and extinguishments under statutory powers the procedure follows a standard pattern. First an order, or a draft order, is made and published; then an opportunity is given for objections and representations to be made to a minister, who, if these are not withdrawn, is normally required to hold a local enquiry. The Minister then decides whether or not to confirm the order (with or without modifications), and his decision has to be published. The order as confirmed is then customarily capable of being challenged by proceedings in the High Court on the ground that any requirement of the Act has not been complied with, or that the order is not within the powers of the Act (see, eg 1980 Act, Sched 2, para 2, applied to orders under ss 118, 119 and 26 (creating public paths) by Sched 6 as amended by Sched 16 to the 1981 Act). This procedure must be instituted within six weeks and is open only to a 'person aggrieved'. This expression is not without ambiguity; it clearly includes someone whose legal interests are affected and possibly includes a person who appeared at the local inquiry (*Turner v Secretary of State for the Environment* (1973) 72 LGR 380), but may not include a person whose only 'interest' is that he regularly walks along the way: *Roberton v Secretary of State for the Environment* [1976] 1 WLR 371 689.

Details may vary, however, in particular cases, and the precise statutory provisions in question should be examined in each case. It will be essential to bring evidence in support of, or to challenge every part of the relevant statutory power relied upon.

The Local Authorities (Recovery of Costs for Public Paths Orders) Regulations 1993 (SI No 407) empower authorities to charge applicants seeking orders (under ss 26, 118, 118A, 119 and 119A of the Highways Act 1980 and ss 257 and 261(2) of the Town and Country Planning Act 1990) for the costs incurred in making the orders. A maximum charge of £400 is laid down where the order relates to one path, with an additional £75 for each further path affected by the order. Guidance on the application of the Regulations is contained in a circular (3/93) issued by the Department of the Environment. The circular advises that relevant costs include those incurred by authorities in:

(1) notifying landowners and other affected persons;

(2) erecting site notices;

(3) undertaking site inspections; and

(4) preparing reports for committees of the local authority

Although local authorities have a discretion whether to impose a charge under the Regulations, the circular acknowledges that most authorities are likely to levy one.

4 Access to highways

It is provided by the Highways Act 1980, s 80(1) that the highway authority may 'erect and maintain fences or posts for the purpose of preventing access' to any highway maintainable at public expense by them. Such fences or posts may subsequently be altered or removed by the authority, but the powers conferred by the section may not be exercised so as to interfere with a fence or gate required for the purpose of agriculture, *obstruct a public right of way*, or obstruct any means of access for which planning permission has been given under the Town and Country Planning Act 1990. A 'public right of way' does not necessarily exist where the public are in the habit of passing; and the question of what constitutes a public right of way may well come into issue in such cases.

In *Marshall v Blackpool Corporation* [1935] AC 16 it was held that it would require very plain words in a local Act to give a right to take away, without compensation, the well-established common law right of an owner of land adjoining a highway (and this includes, of course, a public footpath or bridleway) to access thereto from any part of his premises, the right of the public to pass along the highway being subject to that right of access (but see now the Highways Act 1980, ss 124–128). However, the making of any new access to any highway amounts to development for which, *prima facie*, express planning permission is necessary under the Town and Country Planning Act 1990 (see definition of 'engineering operations' in s 336(1) of that Act). The erection or construction of a gate abutting on a highway used by vehicular traffic where the gate does not exceed 1 metre in height, or 2 metres in any other case, or the formation or laying out of a means of access to any highway which is not a trunk or classified road, is deemed to be 'permitted development' for which express planning permission is not necessary, under the Town and Country Planning General Development Order 1988 (SI No 1813), Sched 2, Part 2, Class A and B.

Chapter 7

Legal Proceedings and Procedure

1 Introduction

The institution and defence of legal proceedings may arise, so far as the scope of this book is concerned, in three principal forms, viz:
- (a) in disputes as to whether public rights of way do or do not exist and if they exist their extent;
- (b) in regard to obstruction of footpaths and other roadways; and
- (c) in questions of liability to repair. It may also be desirable to contest an order diverting or extinguishing an existing right of way (*see* p 76 *et seq*).

The proceedings will sometimes arise between two individuals, one of whom is asserting and the other denying a claim that a certain way is a public highway or that it is being obstructed or that it must be repaired by or at the expense of the other; and at other times one of the parties will be a local authority acting on behalf of the public. Since the passing of the Law Reform (Limitation of Actions etc) Act 1954, local authorities have been in no more privileged a position as defendants in legal proceedings taken against them than are any other litigants, except in so far as they have the resources of the council tax and business rates to finance the proceedings. It is, however, first necessary to explain the extent to which a local highway authority may be held liable to repair or maintain a highway maintainable at the public expense which is vested in them.

2 Non-feasance

Apart from statutory or other special liability, a local authority formerly could not be held liable to pay damages for injury caused by mere neglect to carry out highway repairs for which that authority were responsible. They were liable for acts of *mis-feasance* or *mal-feasance* but not for 'acts' of, or omissions amounting to, *non-feasance*, the leading authority being *Cowley v Newmarket Local Board* [1892] AC 345.

However, this doctrine was abolished by the Highways (Miscellaneous Provisions) Act 1961, since replaced by the Highways Act 1980, s 58. Under this section a highway authority may be sued in respect of damage resulting from their failure to carry out the duty imposed on them by s 41, *ibid*, to maintain any highway vested in them which is maintainable at the public expense. In any such proceedings for damages, the highway authority will be able to plead the special defence (as well as any other defences that may be available to them, such as contributory negligence on the part of the plaintiff) given by the statute (s 58(1)) that they had taken 'such care as in all the circumstances was reasonably required to secure that the part of the highway to which the action relates was not dangerous for traffic'. In determining whether this defence is to succeed in a particular case, the court is required in particular to have regard to matters listed in subs (2), including the character of the highway and the traffic which was reasonably expected to use it.

The proceedings may be brought in the High Court if the value of the claim exceeds £50,000 and in the county court for lower value claims. An example of a High Court Statement of Claim and Defence is at Appendix 2.

There have been a number of decisions of the superior courts (eg *Griffiths v Liverpool Corporation* [1967] 1 QB 374; *Meggs v Liverpool Corporation* (1967) 65 LGR 479; and *Littler v Liverpool Corporation* [1968] 2 All ER 343) by which it seems to have been established, so far as accidents occurring on footways in urban streets are concerned, that whereas the authority may be liable unless it can be shown there was an adequate system of inspection and repair, the standard of repair required is merely such that the way shall not be dangerous. 'The test in relation to a length of pavement is reasonable foreseeability of danger' (*per* Cumming-Bruce J in *Littler's* case, at p 345). These principles apply also, *mutatis mutandis*, to carriageways. Thus, the authority should even be able to foresee that some drivers might make those ordinary mistakes which experience and common sense taught were likely to occur. But, said Sachs LJ in *Rider v Rider* [1973] QB 505, at p 515: 'It is perhaps as well, however, to emphasise my agreement with the manifestly correct view that mere unevenness, undulations, and minor potholes do not normally constitute a danger, and also to say that the normal run of drivers does not include the drunk or the reckless'.

In *Haydon v Kent CC* [1978] QB 343 the plaintiff claimed damages in respect of injuries she sustained from a fall on a footpath which had become very slippery from impacted snow. The snow had fallen three days previously and had not been cleared by the highway authority. Clearance of snow was held by a majority of the Court of Appeal to fall within the duty to maintain, but they held further that no breach of the duty had been established, having regard to the short interval of time between the snowfall and the accident, and that the path was in fact cleared shortly after the accident.

Recently the Court of Appeal has determined the class of plaintiffs who may seek to bring an action for breach of the duty imposed by s 41 of the 1980 Act and the type of damages available. In *Wentworth v Wiltshire County Council* [1993] All ER 256. the plaintiff was a dairy farmer who asserted that a road serving his farm was a highway maintainable at public expense. For 20 years the highway authority had disputed that claim. The road deteriorated to such an extent that in early 1980 the Milk Marketing Board refused to allow their tanker to travel along the road to the plaintiff's farm. Consequently the plaintiff had to give up dairy farming. Later in 1980 the Crown Court, at the request of the plaintiff, determined that the highway authority was under a duty to maintain the road. Subsequently, the plaintiff brought an action alleging that the authority was in breach of its statutory duty to maintain the road and claiming damages for the financial loss incurred through having to give up dairy farming. The High Court upheld his claim and awarded him £77,000 damages. On appeal the Court of Appeal held that:

The 1961 Act affords a cause of action for breach of s 44 of the 1959 Act (now s 41 of the Highways Act 1980) only to a limited class of persons, namely road users who can prove that they have suffered physical injury to person or property as a result of the dangerous condition of the highway through want of repair and maintenance. Section 59 of the 1959 Act (now s 56 of the 1980 Act) provides an adequate and appropriate remedy, and, in my view, the only remedy, for all other persons who wish to complain of the non-repair of the highway, whether or not they suffered or expect to suffer loss consequent thereon (*per* Stuart-Smith LJ at p 268).

Therefore, the High Court's decision was reversed. It is now clear that individuals not personally using a highway cannot bring a claim for non-feasance by a highway authority and even users of highways cannot claim damages for pure economic losses incurred through failures to maintain a highway (significantly the House of Lords refused leave to appeal in the above case).

Owing to the special defences, the change in the law may indeed prove in practice not as revolutionary as might at first appear. The defence of non-feasance was never available to an authority who were not acting as highway authority, and it seems that in such circumstances the special defence of s 58(1) of the 1980 Act also will not be relevant. Thus, if a local authority are acting as sewer authority (*Newsome v Darton Urban District Council* [1938] 3 All ER 93) and they open a trench, they will be liable for damages if they fail to repair the surface properly, and they will generally be liable for creating a nuisance on a highway under powers other than those as a highway authority (See *Skilton v Epsom and Ewell Urban District Council* [1937] 1 KB 112. In these cases, where liability attaches, the local authority will be responsible for the acts of their contractor (See eg *Penny v Wimbledon Urban District Council* [1899] 2 QB 72). Accordingly authorities should ensure that contractual provisions clearly define the responsibility of the contractor so that if the authority is subsequently sued for the contractor's negligence, the authority can rely upon an indemnity from the contractor.

3 Action by local authorities

We have seen (p 68) that the duty of protecting the public interest in rural areas is placed by the 1980 Act on the county councils. The enforcement of rights of way duly recorded on the definitive map prepared under the National Parks and Access to the Countryside Act 1949 or of other rights of way, is also the responsibility of the county council. This duty is not confined to public rights of way actually and wholly within the area of the council concerned; if a public right of way is threatened in an adjoining county and its loss might be prejudicial to the interests of their own district, the council may act under the Highways Act 1980, s 130(5). (The Local Government Act 1972, s 222 may also be relevant on occasion.) Similarly, a district council may act in respect of a highway within or without their own district. A council may take action themselves, or in lieu of so doing they may assist any private person who is maintaining a public right (*ibid*). Such assistance may take the form of a money grant towards his expenses, whether he is plaintiff or defendant. In *R v Norfolk County Council* [1901] 2 KB 268, the district council had declined to assist private litigants in resisting a landowner's claim, and the parish council appealed to the county council for help, which was given. An application to set aside a resolution passed by the county council, transferring the powers and duties of the district council to themselves, was dismissed by the High Court (see also p 70).

There is, therefore, no necessity for any private individual to take action himself in the interests of the public generally. What he should do is to persuade the local authority to act and this, in a rural area, is best done through the intervention of the parish or community council under s 130(6) of the Highways Act 1980 (see p 73). Subject to the caution administered to local authorities in the *Egham* case (see p 71) as to the care they should exercise in deciding whether to take action, there will usually be no difficulty in securing a proper legal investigation into any complaint, and the fact that a particular path may have been missed in the survey under the National Parks and Access to the Countryside Act 1949 or in reviews thereof, need not deter a local authority sure of the facts (see the county court case of *Andover Corporation v Mundy* [1955] JPL 518).

4 Action by private individuals

Although there is no reason why the onus of taking action to enforce what is believed to be a public right should not be placed upon the appropriate local authority, there are cases from time to time in which private individuals may assume responsibility for so doing. 'Where population was increasing,' said Neville J in *Holloway v Egham Urban District Council* (see p 71),

and the value of land was growing, there was a very great danger of public rights being invaded by individual proprietors, who acted in furtherance of their own interests, whereas it was rare to find a member of the public sufficiently wealthy and public-spirited to take proceedings and to fight for the infinitesimal interest that it usually was for him, though it was of much larger interest to the invading landowner.

Although development is today even more rapid the position is largely reversed, and in the great majority of cases it is the land-owner who is called upon to protect his interests against the local authority.

If, therefore, the occasions upon which private individuals defend public interests are now rare, the occasions upon which they are called upon to defend their own interests are numerous, as a result of the surveys under the National Parks and Access to the Countryside Act 1949 and the increased activity of local authorities and associations bent upon establishing and confirming public rights to the fullest extent.

Individuals concerned in such a matter may well be advised to seek the assistance of a local amenity society in establishing the facts (such as, for example, the Ramblers' Association at 1/5 Wandsworth Road, London SW8 2XX or the Byways and Bridleways Trust at The Granary, Charlcutt Calne, Wiltshire SN11 9HL.

5 Right of way or encroachment cases

Section 31 of the Highways Act 1980 (see p 34), has greatly simplified the work of the courts in deciding disputes as to whether or not an alleged public right of way exists over certain land. In *Gloucestershire CC v Farrow* [1984] 1 WLR 262 Goulding J stated that Parliament had enacted s 31, 'in order to avoid the need for lengthy and expensive antiquarian investigations when highway rights are called in question' (at p 270). It lays down certain criteria to enable the court to determine whether a public right of way does or does not exist. Where the facts in question fit in with these criteria, litigation becomes unnecessary if the parties agree as to the facts. These principles are not affected, except to a minor extent, by the passing of the National Parks and Access to the Countryside Act 1949 and they will be applied by local authorities and others concerned with the survey of rights of way and subsequent proceedings under Pt IV of the Act (see p 24 et seq).

The same remedies apply whether the action contemplated is to maintain an alleged public right or to resist a claim to such an alleged right. There are several ways in which legal action may be taken—though the first two are generally included in the same proceedings. The court may be asked for a 'declaration', ie a pronouncement as to whether a particular footpath, bridleway or cartway is or is not a public highway. This is a convenient and often desirable method of procedure, with the advantage that it may encourage a 'friendly' action where both parties are in doubt and where both are prepared to abide by an impartial judicial decision without fighting each other at arms' length. This was obviously the type of procedure in the mind of Lord Russell CJ when he said in *Reynolds v Presteign Urban District Council* [1896] 1 QB 604 that a public body should not be too ready to take the law into their own hands but when the question was one of doubt or difficulty, should obtain a judicial decision upon it. The practice with regard to declarations will be found in RSC Ord 15, r 16 (for further explanation see the Supreme Court Practice; and see *Locke-King v Woking Urban District Council* (1897) 77 LT 790).

The county court now has jurisdiction to grant declaratory relief independently of a claim for damages (Courts and Legal Services Act 1990, s 3 and see the County Court Practice 1993, pp 36–42). Unless the Attorney-General is made a party to the action, as the protector of public rights, any declaration made will bind only the parties to the action and not other members of the public: *Thornhill v Weeks* [1913] 1 Ch 438 and *Newton Abbot Rural District Council v Wills* (1913) 77 JP 333.

As an alternative to (or sometimes joined with) an action for a declaration, an action may be brought for trespass and damages (generally nominal) with an injunction to restrain further trespasses and a declaration as to the rights in issue. This is the type of action which results from the ill-tempered proceedings too often associated with right of way disputes—the erection of a barrier by a landowner who denies the right of the public to pass by, its destruction by an angry crowd, and unseemly repetition of these proceedings day after day until perhaps the police have to interfere to prevent a serious breach of the peace. The erection of a barrier by a landowner to demonstrate what he deems to be his own legal rights, and its formal removal by individuals acting on behalf of the public (or better still by officials of the county council), may, in some cases, be necessary in order to raise legal issues, but all this can be done without any breach of the peace: see also Highways Act 1980, s 31(5); see p 41. County courts have jurisdiction in highway cases which originate in an action for trespass, and such actions should be commenced in the county court, rather than the High Court, if the value of the claim is under £50,000 (Courts and Legal Services Act 1990, s 1 and the High Court and County Courts Jurisdiction Order 1991 (SI No 724)).

The question as to the status of a particular road may also be raised in proceedings in the course of making up a private street at the expense of the frontagers, under Pt XI of the Act of 1980 as amended by the Local Government Act 1985, Sched 4.

If the encroachment is recent it may also constitute an obstruction—as to which, see the following section.

6 Obstruction cases

It is necessary to be quite clear as to what is meant by the word 'obstruction'. It may mean that some obstruction (eg a gate or a fence or barbed wire) is being deliberately set up by an owner or occupier of land for the express purpose of disputing a claim to a public right of way; or it may simply mean that an admitted public way is being made more or less impassable or inconvenient by something deposited on the way, by overgrowth from adjoining hedges, by the existence of a dangerous cavity, or by a variety of other possible causes of complaint. (If barbed wire has been placed on a fence adjoining a highway in such a manner as amounts to a nuisance, the appropriate authority (or Secretary of State) may serve a notice on the occupier of the land requiring its removal. The notice may be enforced on complaint to the local magistrate (Highways Act 1980, s 164).)

All these last-mentioned matters come within the scope of the term 'nuisances', and may be dealt with under the Highways Act 1980. They are distinct from 'right of way' and 'encroachment' cases, and are therefore not relevant to the present inquiry. They may be 'public' nuisances, affecting the community at large, or they may be 'private' nuisances affecting individuals only. The reference in s 130 of the Act of 1980 (see p 70) to 'the stopping up or obstruction' of a right of way refers to cases in which there is a denial of the public right of passage which is claimed. It is unfortunate that the word 'obstruction' is so often used to indicate what is known legally as a nuisance; and the distinction therefore needs to be made clear. The 1980 Act contains ample provisions for dealing with ordinary obstructions and nuisances (see s 131) and the provisions left unrepealed of the Highway Act 1835, s 72 (note: the penalty for these offences was increased in severity by the Criminal Justice Act 1982, Sched 3) and (in urban areas) the Town Police Clauses Act 1847, s 28, applied generally by the Public Health Act 1875, s 171. As to ploughing up, see p 59.

Additionally, s 137(1) of the Highways Act 1980 makes it a criminal offence for a person to 'wilfully obstruct' a highway. The elements of this offence were re-stated in a modern case involving a farmer who had erected a gate across a bridleway in order to prevent his livestock straying onto the adjacent highway. In *Durham County Council v Scott* [1991] JPL 362 the High Court held that the authorities provided:

. . . the correct approach for justices who are dealing with the issues which arose, and arise in the present case, is as follows. First, they should consider: is there an obstruction? Unless the obstruction is so small that one can consider it comes within the rubric *de minimis*, any stopping on the highway, whether it be on the carriageway or on the footway, is *prima facie* an obstruction. To quote Lord Parker: 'Any occupation of part of a road, thus interfering with people having the use of the whole of the road, is an obstruction'. The second question then will arise: was it wilful, that is to say, deliberate? Clearly, in many cases a pedestrian or a motorist has to stop because the traffic lights are against the motorist or there are other people in the way, not because he wishes to do so. Such stopping is not wilful. But if the stopping is deliberate, then there is wilful obstruction. Then there arises the third question: have the prosecution proved that the obstruction was without lawful authority or excuse? Lawful authority includes permits and licences granted under statutory provision, as I have already said, such as for market and street traders and, no doubt, for those collecting for charitable causes on Saturday mornings. Lawful excuse embraces activities otherwise lawful in themselves, which may or may not be reasonable in all the circumstances . . . (at p 363).

The Court found that the gate, although easily opened, prevented users of the bridleway from having free acess over the whole right of way, the gate had been in place for 15 years, and placing a gate across the bridleway was not a reasonable user of the highway; therefore, the farmer was guilty of wilful obstruction.

A specimen Information and Summons alleging an offence under s 137 of the 1980 Act is included at Appendix 3. It is essential to be able to prove all of the matters relating to the offence as illustrated by the decision of the court in *Durham County Council v Scott* (above). The threat of prosecution can often be sufficient to persuade those responsible to remove obstructions.

A bull in a field crossed by a public right of way may constitute a special form of obstruction. Formerly this matter was regulated in some counties by local byelaws. Now s 59 of the Act of 1981 makes provision for the whole country.

By this section, it is made an offence punishable by a fine not exceeding £200, if the occupier of a field or enclosure crossed by a public right of way permits a bull to be at large except:

(1) if the bull does not exceed the age of ten months; or
(2) if the bull is not of a recognised dairy breed and is at large in any field or inclosure in which cows or heifers are at large.

'Recognised dairy breed' for this purpose means one of the following breeds: Ayrshire, British Friesian, British Holstein, Dairy Short-horn, Guernsey, Jersey and Kerry. This list may be added to by order made by the Secretary of State by statutory instrument, which will be subject to the negative resolution procedure (s 59(4), (5)).

7 Issues and evidence

As has been pointed out (see p 35 *et seq*), the Highways Act 1980, s 31 and its predecessors have greatly simplified procedure by limiting the issues in a right of way dispute, and it is no longer necessary in many cases to produce a succession of 'oldest inhabitants' to entertain the court with their reminiscences. The issues may be summarised briefly. The claimant must prove that:

(1) the way had been used by the public for 20 years before the right of user was challenged;

(2) such user was 'as of right' (see p 37); and

(3) it was enjoyed without interruption throughout (see p 38).

The above, if accepted by the court, will suffice to establish a *prima facie* case in favour of dedication. To rebut this, the owner must prove one at least of the following:

(1) that the user was conditional (see p 37); or

(2) that user was not as of right on the part of all the Queen's subjects, but permissive; or

(3) that it was effectively interrupted; or

(4) that there was no intention during that period to dedicate (see p 41).

As to the evidence that may be adduced to prove (or disprove) these matters, s 32 of the 1980 Act provides as follows:

A court or other tribunal, before determining whether a way has or has not been dedicated as a highway, or the date on which such dedication, if any, took place, shall take into consideration any map, plan or history of the locality or other relevant document which is tendered in evidence, and shall give such weight thereto as the court or tribunal considers justified by the circumstances, including the antiquity of the tendered document, the status of the person by whom and the purpose for which it was made or compiled, and the custody in which it has been kept and from which it is produced.

This section makes extensive inroads into the rules of evidence formerly applicable to the determination of right of way disputes. Under this provision the court must admit any 'map, plan, history, or other relevant document' tendered by either side to the dispute. Having admitted the document, the court is allowed absolute discretion as to the weight to be attached to it having regard to all the circumstances connected with its publication, its production in the proceedings, and the status of its author. The section is silent as to how evidence of 'status' is to be given. Presumably that will in most cases be inferred from the general quality of the document itself, unless the author may himself be a personage known to fame.

Footpaths that have been established in the definitive map are now shown in red on many of the maps issued by the Ordnance Survey, but the warning on these maps to the effect that the representation on the map of other tracks, etc, is no evidence of the existence of a right of way, should be remembered; but even in respect of these other tracks or paths the map is evidence of the physical features existing as at the date of the survey (*Att-Gen v Meyrick and Jones* (1915) 79 JP 515). The definitive maps themselves where appropriate, rather than Ordnance Survey maps, should be used in legal proceedings (and see below).

The value of maps generally as evidence was discussed in *Merstham Manor Ltd v Coulsdon and Purley Urban District Council* (see p 37). Hilbery J in his judgment, said ([1936] 2 All ER 422, at p 438):

It is not necessary, I think, to discuss the ancient maps, the ordnance maps, the tithe maps and the estate maps, save to say this. The road is shown as a road on the earliest maps put in evidence before me. Rocque's map of 1762, produced from the custody of the British Museum . . . was the earliest in date. It showed the road in question and the shaw alongside which it runs. The road is again shown [in maps of] 1802, 1822 and 1823; but, of course, these maps only show it as a road. There is nothing in the maps to show whether or not the topographer-author was intending to represent the roads on his map as public highways. All the ordnance survey maps show the road; but it was admitted by . . . a witness from the Ordnance Survey Department that they show any road which is there on the surface whether it is a public highway or not. The tithe maps make no distinction between a public and a private road; their object is to show what is titheable, and the roadways are marked upon them as untitheable parts of the land whether they are public or private . . . I do not find that they give me any assistance in arriving at the conclusions to which I have come.

Even apart from s 32 of the 1980 Act, maps have been admitted in evidence in this type of dispute: see, eg *Vyner v Wirrall Rural District Council* (1909) 73 JP 242, and *Copestake v West Sussex County Council* [1911] 2 Ch 331.

Once a definitive map has been settled for the whole of the area the opportunities for dispute as to the status of any public path shown thereon will be few (1981 Act, s 56), but new paths may be claimed on application for a modification order under s 53 *ibid*, or under the older procedure (*Att-Gen v Honeywill* [1972] 1 WLR 1506; *Andover Corporation v Mundy* [1955] JPL 518) and see p 31.

8 Proof of dedication from user

The correct method of proving dedication from user was laid down by Lord Kinnear in *Folkestone Corporation v Brockman* [1914] AC at p 352, as follows:

Dedication, in my opinion, is matter of fact . . . The nature of user, and consequently the weight to be given to it, varies indefinitely in different cases, and whether it will import a presumption of grant or dedication must depend upon the circumstances of the particular case. The law is stated more exactly by Lord Blackburn in *Mann v Brodie* (1885) 10 App Cas 378, at p 386. He begins by citing the doctrine laid down by Parke B in *Poole v Huskinson* (1843) 11 M & W 827, at p 830: 'In order to constitute a valid dedication to the public of a highway by the owner of the soil, it is clearly settled that there must be an intention to dedicate—there must be an *animus dedicandi*, of which the user by the public is evidence and no more'. And then he adds more particularly with reference to the effect of user, that 'where there has been evidence of user by the public so long and in such a manner that the owner of the fee, whoever he was, must have been aware that the public were acting under the belief that the way had been dedicated, and has taken no steps to disabuse them of that belief, it is not conclusive evidence, but evidence on which those who have to find that fact may find that there was a dedication by the owner, whoever he was'.

The points to be noted are, first, that the thing to be proved is intention to dedicate, and secondly, that while public user may be evidence tending to instruct dedication, it will be good for that purpose only when it is exercised under such conditions as to imply the assertion of a right, within the knowledge and with the acquiescence of the owner of the fee. The cases in which the law is stated in the same way are numerous, but I refer to one in particular in which it was so laid down by Lord Chancellor Halsbury, *Macpherson v Scottish Rights of Way and Recreation Society* (1888) 13 App Cas 744, because I think his Lordship's observations bring out very sharply the determining fact of which in a case like the present the judges of fact must be satisfied, before they can find room for the application of any presumption of law. The law of Scotland as to rights of way differs from that of England in this respect, that the public right, as Lord Watson more fully explains in *Mann v Brodie* (1885) 10 App Cas 378, is not rested upon any theory of dedication, but upon acquisitive prescription; but the two laws agree in this, that the public use from which a right of way is to be inferred must be had as of right. With reference to this difference, the Lord Chancellor says: 'The question in the mind of an English lawyer is not only whether he can, on proper judicial evidence, determine that there has been an exercise of such a right of way as is here in question, but whether he can reasonably infer that the owner had a real intention of dedicating that way to the use of the public. That, however, is not the law of Scotland; and if it can be established that for the necessary period there has in fact been such a use of the way as negatives a mere licence or permission, then, as I understand the law of Scotland, that establishes absolutely the right of way in question'.

This extract from Lord Kinnear's speech was quoted *in extenso* by Hilbery J in *Merstham Manor Ltd v Coulsdon and Purley Urban District Council* [1937] 2 KB 77, at p 79. In *Att-Gen (ex p Weymouth Corporation) v Bird* (1936) *The Times*, 9 July (a case referred from the Chancery Division to the Official Referee owing to the number of local witnesses), it was found as a fact that a path along some cliffs had, throughout living memory, been plainly visible and frequently used by the public, and also that the right of way was enjoyed as of right and without interruption over the period of living memory up to 1930, when the defendant objected to the user. It was held that the user was good evidence of intention to dedicate to the public made before living memory and that there was a dedication. It was also held that, as the condition of s 1(2) of the 1932 Act (since repealed by the National Parks and Access to the Countryside Act 1949, s 58) had been fulfilled up to 1930, a public right of way under that section had been established.

9 Repair cases

The nature of the legal proceedings available to enforce the liability to repair of a private individual or body or of a local authority who are neglecting their duty used to depend upon the circumstances. There were formerly three different methods available. These were summary procedure under the Highways Acts; the antiquated method of indictment at quarter sessions or assizes; and High Court proceedings. It may also be possible to sue for damages if injury has been sustained as a consequence of a failure to 'maintain' the way (see p 84).

(a) Procedure under the Highway Acts

The Highway Act 1835 (ss 94, 95) provided that the local justices, upon complaint and information, might summon the surveyor 'or other person or body politic or corporate' chargeable with repairs and make an order for the repairs to be carried out within a specified time.

This, and other provisions in pre-1959 legislation, have been repealed and a new enforcement procedure has been provided by the Highways Act 1980, s 56. Under this section any complainant may serve a notice on the highway authority (or private individual who is liable to maintain the highway) requiring the respondent to state whether it is admitted that the way (or bridge) is a highway and that he is liable to maintain it. If this is not admitted within one month, the complainant may apply to the crown court for an order requiring the respondent to put the way into proper repair within a reasonable period. If the respondent does so admit within one month, the complainant may obtain a similar order from the local magistrates. Thus, if there is a dispute as to the status of the way or the responsibility for maintenance, this falls to be decided by the crown court, but if any dispute is confined to the condition of the way, this is determined by the magistrates (and see p 56). If the authority do not admit liability to maintain the way, it is important that the counternotice is most carefully drafted and the one month time limit observed.

Where a person or body sought to be compelled is liable *ratione tenuræ* (see p 51), a simple and effective method of compulsion is provided by the Highways Act 1980, s 57(2). By that subsection, upon failure on the part of the person or body liable to repair, the highway authority may carry out the repairs and sue the person liable to maintain the highway for the cost (see *Daventry Rural District Council v Parker* [1900] 1 QB 1, decided on a corresponding provision in earlier legislation).

There is now also a special procedure for enforcement of the statutory duty to repair stiles and gates, under the 1980 Act, s 146 (see p 57).

(b) Procedure by indictment

This was, in form, a criminal proceeding, based on the principle that non-repair of a highway was an offence against the Crown. It was abolished by s 59(1) of the 1959 Act.

(c) High Court proceedings

Formerly it was possible for a plaintiff to take proceedings in the High Court in the name of the Attorney-General and ask for a declaration of liability and possibly a mandatory order for repairs. This form of procedure has not been abolished by the Acts of 1959 and 1980, but as the consent of the Attorney-General has to be obtained, and the court has a wide discretion in proceedings for a declaration or an injunction, it seems unlikely that either the Attorney-General's consent or the court's order would be granted in any case where the statutory procedure is available.

Chapter 8

Public Rights over Commons and the Countryside

1 Introduction

Closely bound up with the subject of public rights of way is the question of public rights to traverse commons, manorial wastes, mountain and forest tracts and other desirable places of resort under private or public ownership—'open country', in the language of the National Parks and Access to the Countryside Act 1949, Pt V, or 'countryside', in the more modern Countryside Act 1968. Such areas, if under public control or ownership, are, as a rule, subject to clearly defined regulations. If the land is used for military or like purposes, regulations as to the public user are issued by the official department concerned; if it belongs to the National Trust or to the Nature Conservancy Council (now known as English Nature: Environmental Protection Act 1990, Part VII) (under the National Parks and Access to the Countryside Act 1949) access, where allowed, will be subject to the appropriate regulations. (In these cases, public rights of access are usually very limited in extent, if they exist at all.) With these, therefore, it is not our present purpose to deal; nor are we here concerned with commons or commonable rights as affecting persons known as 'commoners'. We are merely concerned with the rights of the public at large to traverse the lands described which are in *private* ownership and to which, until recent years, no right of access has been recognised by law—although many great landowners have been generous towards the holiday-making public by disregarding what may have been technically trespass, so long as no destruction of trees or disturbance of game or incendiarism resulted.

2 Early provisions

Prior to the passing of the Law of Property Act 1925 the only persons directly interested in the subject of commons were the landowners and the commoners whose rights were derived from the owners. So far as the public were concerned, their interests were awakened only in the early part of the nineteenth century, when inclosure of common lands by private individuals came into prominence, and the legislature took steps to check the activities of the 'land-snatcher'.

The Inclosure Acts of 1836 and 1845, in sections since repealed by the Commons Act 1876, contained the earliest recorded statutory provisions restricting the enclosure of commons near large towns and of village greens, in the public interest, and made provision to meet the need for recreation grounds, allotments and other improvements of the same kind for the benefit of local inhabitants. The Metropolitan Commons Act 1866 which made provision for the taking over and management by commissioners of commons within the Metropolitan Police District, led to the passing ten years later of the Commons Act 1876 which dealt with commons outside the Metropolitan area.

This important measure empowered the Inclosure Commissioners by provisional order to authorise the inclosure of commons to be managed by conservators upon such terms as they deemed expedient, having regard as well to the health, comfort and convenience of the inhabitants of any cities, towns, villages, or populous places in or near any parish in which the land proposed to be inclosed lay, as to the advantage of the private interests of the persons concerned. The public interests to be provided for were:

(a) free access;

(b) trees and objects of historical interest to be preserved;

(c) recreation grounds to be provided;

(d) carriage roads, bridlepaths and footways to be laid out; and

(e) other specified things to be done which might be equitable or expedient, regard being had to the benefit of the neighbourhood.

In 1845 the Lands Clauses Consolidation Act had provided special machinery for the acquisition of common lands at a time when railway development was in full swing. Thereafter the Inclosure Act 1845 and a series of statutes dealing with public health and local government, were passed enabling local authorities to purchase and otherwise acquire and hold commons and open spaces for the public benefit, until the Commons Act 1899 supplementing the provisions of the Local Government Act 1894 made ample provision for public acquisition by all local authorities of lands suitable for public recreation. Under the provisions of the 1894 Act (s 26(2)), it became the duty of district councils, with the consent of the county council, to assist the public in maintaining rights of common where, in their opinion, the extinction of such rights was threatened and would prejudice the rights of local inhabitants. (As to schemes for the management of the commons under this Act, see the Commons Regulations 1935 (SR & O 1935 No 840). This subsection has not been repealed by the Highways Act 1959 or 1980 or by the Local Government Act 1972; the reference in the 1894 Act to district councils must now be read as referring to the district councils created by the 1972 Act.) Local authorities and government departments wishing to acquire land forming part of a common have to follow the 'special parliamentary procedure' laid down in the Statutory Orders (Special Procedure) Act 1945 (Acquisition of Land Act 1981, s 19).

3 Law of Property Act 1925

The Law of Property Act 1925 provided that there should be a public right of access 'for air and exercise' to:
  (1) all commons within the meaning of the Metropolitan Commons Acts 1866 to 1898, ie 'any common the whole or any part of which is situate within the Metropolitan Police District' (Metropolitan Commons Act 1866, s 4. As to the limits of the police district, see Metropolitan Police Act 1839, s 2, which prescribes the district as being any part of the Central Criminal Court District or any parish not more than 15 miles from Charing Cross included by subsequent Order);
  (2) any manorial waste or common which, immediately before 1 April 1974, was wholly or partly situated within a borough or urban district; and
  (3) any land which formed a common at the time the Act came into operation and which the lord of the manor or other owner might, by legal process, place under the terms of the Act (1925 Act, s 193(1), as amended by the Local Government Act 1972, s 189(4) and the Local Government Act 1985, Sched 8).
The 1925 Act gave only 'rights of access', which, it is submitted,

amount to nothing more than a right of walking to and fro on the common. Any rights to drive vehicles on the common or to camp or light any fire thereon are expressly excluded (s 193(1) proviso (c)), and indeed it is made an offence to do any of these acts 'without lawful authority' (s 193(4)); how 'lawful authority' to camp on a common could be acquired does not appear. Further, the Act can only be applied to commons within class (c), above, on the initiative of 'the lord of the manor or other person entitled to the soil' of the land; no local or other public authority is given any compulsory powers. Byelaws and schemes for the regulation of commons may be made under the Commons Act 1899, s 1 and see the Commons (Schemes) Regulations 1982 (SI No 209), but not under the present section. (Schemes made under the Metropolitan Commons Amendment Act 1869 and other statutes have been subject to judicial interpretation. See *Cook v Mitcham Common Conservators* [1901] 1 Ch 387; and *Chislehurst Common Conservators v Newton* [1901] 1 Ch 389 (case heard in 1887, but reported as a note to the foregoing case); *Mitcham Common Conservators v Cox* [1911] 2 KB 854, and *Harris v Harrison* (1914) 30 TLR 532.)

4 National Parks and Access to the Countryside Act 1949

The National Parks and Access to the Countryside Act 1949 had as one of its main objects 'securing access to open country', and the whole of Pt V is devoted to that object. Only a brief summary of this Part of the Act can be attempted here, but it should first be emphasised that Pt V applies only to 'open country' as defined by s 59(2), now supplemented by the Countryside Act 1968, s 16, ie an area consisting 'wholly or predominantly of mountain, moor, heath, down, cliff or foreshore (including any bank, barrier, dune, beach, flat or other land adjacent to the foreshore)', but also including any woodlands, and any river or canal 'in the countryside' (an expression which is not itself defined) and also expanses of water and river banks (see s 16 of the 1968 Act).

First, the county planning authority (see the Local Government Act 1972, Sched 17, paras 35–37) must make a general survey of the 'access requirements' of the area, and then take steps to secure rights of access for the public 'for open-air recreation' to land which falls within the definition of 'open country'. This they may do by:

(1) making an 'access agreement' with the landowner(s) (s 64 of

the 1949 Act), and imposing conditions therein under the Countryside Act 1968, s 18; any such agreement may be made binding on successors in title to the parties thereto (1968 Act, s 45, and s 66 of the 1949 Act);

(2) making access agreements or access orders in relation to certain waterways owned or managed by the British Waterways Board (Transport Act 1968, s 111);

(3) making a compulsory 'access order' (s 65), in respect of which compensation may be payable (s 70); and

(4) acquiring the land themselves and making it available to the public, the acquisition being either compulsorily or by agreement (s 76).

When such rights have been secured (and the boundaries of the land affected may be indicated by boundary notices erected by the planning authority (s 81)), members of the public entering the land 'for the purpose of open-air recreation', and not doing any damage or contravening any restrictions applying to the particular land under the access agreement or order, cannot be treated as trespassers (s 60), provided also they keep off 'excepted land', ie buildings, land under the plough, and commons, etc; *see* s 60(5), *but see* the exceptions to that subsection in the Countryside Act 1968, s 17. The landowners may not interfere with the rights of the public (s 66), but the use by the public of any way across land subject to an access agreement or access order may not be used to establish the dedication of a highway, the grant of an easement, or the acquisition of an easement by prescription (s 66(4)). This latter rule is particularly important, as the access agreement or access order may provide for a 'sufficient means of access' to the land subject to the agreement or order to be available for the public (s 67), and the planning authority may, if necessary, enforce such rights of access (s 68).

These powers of ensuring access to open country will be used fully in the areas of the 'National Parks', established by the Countryside Commission under Pt II of the 1949 Act. Within the National Parks further special powers exist, such as those given by s 12 to provide accommodation, meals, refreshments, camping sites and parking places for members of the public. Similar powers exist in relation to areas designated as being of outstanding natural beauty (*see* the 1949 Act, ss 87, 88). A county planning committee may make grants or loans in respect of a National Park in order (*inter alia*) to promote its enjoyment by the public (Wildlife and Countryside Act 1981, s 44).

5 Countryside Act 1968

This is perhaps the most far reaching of the statutes providing for public enjoyment of the countryside. When introducing the Bill in the House of Lords (*Hansard*, 18 May 1966, col 988), Lord Kennet said:

We have to think, all at the same time, of next year's harvest, of next year's breeding grounds for the peregrine falcon, of the new towns or districts of towns which we shall need in 1975, of where the water is to come from in 1985 and where the timber is to come from in 2050. Then, with all these we have to think of next weekend's motorists coming out of the city to enjoy themselves in the best of all possible ways, by breathing the fresh air and getting some sun on them.

The Act first lays down general principles: the Countryside Commission (in Wales, the Countryside Council for Wales) is required to keep under review, and to encourage, assist, concert or promote the implementation of any proposals relating to the provision and improvement of facilities for the enjoyment of the countryside, the conservation and enhancement of its natural beauty and amenity, and the need to secure public access to the countryside for the purposes of open-air recreation (s 2 as amended by the Wildlife and Countryside Act 1981, s 72(7)). Further, 'in the exercise of their functions relating to land under any enactment every Minister, government department and public body [an expression which includes local authorities and statutory undertakings] shall have regard to the desirability of conserving the natural beauty and amenity of the countryside' (s 11).

By way of implementing these general principles, the Act includes the following substantive provisions:

(1) The Countryside Commission is given power to formulate experimental projects and schemes to facilitate the enjoyment of the countryside or to conserve or enhance its natural beauty or amenity (s 4 as strengthened by s 40 of the Wildlife and Countryside Act 1981).

(2) Local authorities are empowered to create 'country parks' and to equip them with facilities for open-air recreation, such as sailing, boating, bathing and fishing (see ss 6–8). These country parks are expected to be in the countryside, and they will not be enlarged town recreation grounds; they will be more like Box Hill than Clapham Common. Lord Brooke in the House of Lords made the apt comment that Kubla Khan

was decreeing the provision of a country park in Xanadu (*Hansard*, 25 April 1966, at col 781).

(3) Local authorities may also provide camping sites 'for holiday and recreational purposes' (s 10).

(4) Byelaws may be made by the local authority for the control of boats on any lake in a National Park (s 13).

(5) Powers are given to statutory water undertakers to make their reservoirs and waterways open to members of the public for recreational purposes if it seems reasonable to the undertakers to do so (s 22).

(6) The Forestry Commissioners are empowered to provide tourist, recreational or sporting facilities on any of their land (s 23 as amended by the Forestry Act 1981).

(7) Local authorities are empowered to make byelaws relating to wardens in country parks or at picnic sites provided by the authority (s 41).

6 Wildlife and Countryside Act 1981 (Part II)

Part II of the 1981 Act, which fully came into force in 1982 (SI No 1136) gives power to the Secretary of State to make orders protecting areas of special scientific interest (also the Wildlife and Countryside (Amendment) Act 1985, s 2), to designate national and marine nature reserves, to protect areas of 'limestone pavement', and also moor and heath land in the National Parks. In addition, the Secretary of State or the local authority may enter into a management agreement with the owner or occupier of any land in the countryside, for the purpose of preserving or enhancing the natural beauty of the land, or of promoting its enjoyment by the public. This latter power has been extended to cover the creation of management agreements over environmentally sensitive areas between the owner and the Secretary of State. Under the terms of the Agriculture Act 1986, s 18 the Secretary of State may make payments in consideration of the owner managing the designated land so as to conserve, *inter alia*, its flora, fauna, geological or physiographical features.

7 Ancient Monuments and Archaeological Areas Act 1979

Section 19 of this Act provides that the public shall have access to any monument that is owned by or under the guardianship of the Secretary of State for the Environment, the Historic Buildings and Monuments Commission for England, commonly known as 'English Heritage' (see the National Heritage Act 1983, Sched 4) or a local authority. 'Monument' for the purposes of the Act has an elaborate definition (see s 61(7)) and includes a building, structure or work, cave or excavation and any machinery or plant attached to such a building, etc. The Secretary of State has a duty to schedule ancient monuments and any monument which he after consultation with the Commission considers to be 'of national importance' (s 1(3)). In *R v Secretary of State for the Environment, ex p Rose Theatre Trust Co* [1990] 1 All ER 754, the High Court held that an amenity group formed to campaign for the preservation of the ruins of the Elizabethan Rose Theatre did not have *locus standi*, under RSC Ord 53, to seek judicial review of the Secretary of State's decision not to schedule those ruins under s 1(3) of the 1979 Act. This decision has received much criticism for the restrictive approach taken towards the standing of pressure groups by the court (see eg Cane [1990] *Public Law* 307). Any scheduled monument may then be taken into public ownership or put under guardianship (in the latter case, ownership remains in private hands) either by the Secretary of State, the Commission or by the local authority.

Not all scheduled monuments are owned as above or under guardianship, and the public have no rights of access to them, although private owners may admit members of the public. Where a monument is publicly owned or under public guardianship, the rights of access of the public are subject to the following restrictions:

(1) The Secretary of State, the Commission or local authority may regulate the normal times at which the public will be admitted.

(2) The public may be excluded from access to a monument or any part of it in the interests of safety or for the maintenance or preservation of the monument, by the Secretary of State, the Commission or by the local authority with the approval of the Secretary of State (if the exclusion is on the grounds of preservation).

(3) General regulations may be made applying to all (or specified)

monuments by the Secretary of State (after consultation with the Commission) or the local authority.

(4) Charges for admission may be specified in the regulations.

(5) Individuals may be excluded by an authorised person, if he has reasonable cause to believe that the person excluded is likely to do anything which would tend to injure or disfigure the monument or its amenities, or to disturb the public in their enjoyment of it.

Regulations made by a local authority are subject to confirmation by the Secretary of State (s 19(8)).

In addition, the Secretary of State, the Commission or the local authority may provide facilities and information or other services, and make charges for their use, in connection with access by the public to a monument, either in or on the monument itself, or on land associated with the monument.

Areas of archaeological importance may be specially designated by the Secretary of State as archaeological areas, but this does not give members of the public any rights of access. The use of metal detectors in a 'protected place' without the written consent of the Secretary of State constitutes an offence. A 'protected place' is an area of archaeological importance or the site of a scheduled monument or one owned by the Secretary of State or a local authority or under guardianship, as provided for in the Act.

8 Special cases

For other provisions for access to places for health and recreation and to places of interest, see the Open Spaces Act 1906. The National Trust have wide statutory powers to hold 'inalienable' land, and local authorities may give land to them for those purposes, or may agree with the Trust for the management of an area of land (National Trust Acts 1907, s 31 and 1937, s 7). Local authorities may make grants towards the upkeep of historic buildings or of any garden occupied with such a building and contiguous or adjacent thereto: Local Authorities (Historic Buildings) Act 1962. English Heritage may make grants for the repair of buildings in 'town schemes' (s 80 of the Planning (Listed Buildings and Conservation Areas) Act 1990). The Planning (Listed Buildings and Conservation Areas) Act 1990, with its power to designate conservation areas (Part II) and the tight controls over buildings of special architectural or historic interest is relevant to but beyond the scope of this work.

Tree preservation orders may be made under the Town and Country Planning Act 1990, s 198, and provisions for compensation to be paid where re-planting is required when a woodland area is felled are to be found in the Countryside Act 1968, s 25. General provisions as to the need for considering tree planting are now contained in s 197 of the 1990 Act.

Chapter 9

Private Rights of Way

1 Introduction

The distinction between a 'public' and a 'private' right of way is that the former right is common to all subjects of the Queen, whereas the latter is a right vested in some particular individual or individuals and not in the public at large. According to the learned author of the 'Easements' section of 'Halsbury' (4th edn, vol 14, p 68), a private right of way may be defined as 'a right to utilise the servient tenement as a means of access to or egress from the dominant tenement for some purpose connected with the enjoyment of the dominant tenement, according to the nature of that tenement'. The cases of *Ballard v Dyson* (1808) 1 Taunt 279 and *Cannon* v *Villars* (1878) 8 ChD 415 are cited as containing the judicial dicta from which the nature of a private right of way may be gathered.

The essential qualities of any easement (including a private right of way) have been described in *Re Ellenborough Park* [1956] Ch 131 as being that:

(a) there must be a dominant and a servient tenement;
(b) an easement must accommodate the dominant tenement, ie, be connected with its enjoyment and for its benefit;
(c) the dominant and servient owners must be different persons; and
(d) the right claimed must be capable of forming the subject-matter of a grant (*per* Danckwerts J at p 140, upheld in the Court of Appeal at [1956] Ch 153).

For a more comprehensive analysis of the modern case law on easements see J F Garner 127 SJ 95 and 115.

However, an easement or alleged right of way may not amount to a claim to possession or joint possession of the servient tenement. Thus a claim to dump numbers of different articles on the servient land was held to amount to a claim to exclusive possession and was therefore not capable of subsisting as an easement (*Copeland v Greenhalf* [1952] 1 All ER 809), but a right to enter on the servient land for the purpose of maintaining the plaintiff's wall was capable of subsisting as an easement (see *Ward v Kirkland* [1967] Ch 194; see also the Access to Neighbouring Land Act 1992, below p 123).

2 Extent of user

It was said by the court in *Woodyer v Hadden* (1813) 5 Taunt 125, that a public road differs from a private road in that an occupier may make an opening in his fence and go into it at any part of the length of the public road, or at the end, but in a private road the person entitled to use it must enter at the usual and accustomed part. This must now be read in conjunction with the provisions of the Town and Country Planning Act 1990 as to means of access, though the distinction still holds good as regards private rights of way.

3 Purposes for which a right may be enjoyed

Private rights of way are never general (see p 4). They are always limited to user by the particular persons who are entitled to exercise them. The user may further be limited in regard to
- (a) time;
- (b) season;
- (c) duration;
- (d) class of traffic; or
- (e) mode of user.

It may be restricted to individuals or to specified classes of persons, or to special purposes incidental to its position or nature. The limitations of the grant (express or implied) must not be exceeded. Moreover, the courts have jurisdiction to control the use of a right of way by means of injunctive relief where such an order is necessary to prevent an unreasonable and excessive user (*Rosling v Pinnegar* (1987) 54 P & CR 124). As to the interpretation placed on such grants, see *Hurt v Bowmer* [1937] 1 All ER 797, where it was held that the words 'as at present used' referred merely to the quality of the user and not to the quantity.

In *Ballard v Dyson* (see above), a claim of right was set up to pass and repass with cattle from a public street through and along a certain yard to premises in the plaintiff's occupation as appurtenant thereto. (A claim of prescriptive right of way must always be laid as 'appurtenant to' or 'appendant to' land and not as being annexed to it for a period of years: *Wheaton v Maple & Co* [1893] 3 Ch 48; see also the Law of Property Act 1925, s 62.) From being originally a barn, the 'premises' had become a stable, then a slaughterhouse for pigs, and ultimately (under the plaintiff) for oxen. The 'yard' was a narrow passage with small houses fronting each side. No deed of grant was produced in evidence, and the defendant admitted a right of way for all manner of carriages; this, the plaintiff contended, of necessity included a right of way for all manner of cattle. The jury found for the defendant and on appeal the court refused to disturb the verdict:

This is a prescription for a way for cattle and a carriageway is proved. A carriageway will comprehend a horseway, but not a driftway. All prescriptions are *stricti juris*. Some prescriptions are for a way to market, others of a way to church, and in the ancient entries . . . the pleadings are very particular in stating their claims . . . The usage in this case is evidence of a very different grant from that which is claimed, namely, to drive fat oxen, animals dangerous in their nature, and which there might be very good reason to except out of a grant of a way through a closely inhabited neighbourhood (per Heath J).

This is the case of a prescriptive private way which presumes a grant: the question then is, what was the grant in this case? That is to be collected from the use; for it is to be presumed that the use has been according to the grant. A grant of a carriageway has not always been taken to include a driftway . . . The use proved here is of a carriageway; the grant is not shown and the extent of it can only be known from the use. If the use had been confined to a carriageway, I should have had no difficulty whatever in saying that it afforded no evidence of a way for horned cattle; for till they were driven there no opposition could be made, nor the limitation of the right shown; but pigs have been driven that way and stress is laid upon this circumstance. That then may be good proof of a right that way, but the user of the way for pigs is not proof of a right of way for oxen. The grantor might well consider what animals it was proper to admit and what not. The place is very narrow and full of inhabitants. There is no danger from pigs and carriages have always someone to conduct them. Cattle may do harm and passengers cannot always get out of their way, but if the cattle are driven forward serious injury may be done. The nature of the place, therefore, may probably have suggested a limitation of the grant (per Lawrence J).

The effect of this decision is that where one particular private right of way has been established it does not necessarily include any other right. Proof of one right cannot afford more than presumptive evidence of another right of equal or inferior degree (see *Gale on Easements* 15th ed, p 286 *et seq*, where this case is exhaustively treated, and subsequent cases on the same point are reviewed. Compare this decision with the position as respects public rights of way (see p 4 et seq)).

As with public rights of way, the right given by a private right of way is normally limited to passing and repassing (*London and Suburban Land and Building Co (Holdings) Ltd v Carey* (1991) 62 P & CR 480), but a particular grant may be wider and give rights, eg to halt vehicles on the way for the purpose of loading and unloading, etc (*Bulstrode v Lambert* [1953] 1 WLR 1064; and *McIlraith v Grady* [1968] 1 QB 468).

In *Lock v Abercester Ltd* [1939] Ch 861, it was held as a matter of law that a private right of way acquired for horsedrawn vehicles enabled the owner of the dominant tenement to use the way for mechanically propelled vehicles. Bennett J said: 'As a matter of law I propose to decide that where proof is given of the user of a way by carriages drawn by horses for the required period so as to establish the right to an easement for carriageway, the right so acquired is one which enables the owner of the dominant tenement to use the way with mechanically propelled vehicles'. The learned judge declined to accede to an argument that to establish a way for mechanically propelled vehicles proof of user by such vehicles for the prescribed period was necessary. This decision was followed in *Kain v Norfolk and Baker (Hauliers) Ltd* [1949] Ch 163, when a grant of a right of way for 'carts' referred to a vehicle adapted to carry materials and goods, and the particular mode of propulsion of the cart was held to be immaterial; therefore use of the way by motor lorries was not excessive.

The user made of the servient tenement must not be such as to put a burden thereon different in kind from that contemplated in the grant, even if the words of grant are wide (*Jelbert v Davies* [1968] 1 WLR 589 and *National Trust v White* [1987] 1 WLR 907). Similarly, where the claim to the right of way is based on prescriptive user, the use made may not exceed that which it is claimed (and can be established) was being made throughout the period of prescription. Intensification of use may amount to an unacceptable burden if it is so drastic as to amount almost to a difference in kind, as was suggested in *Cargill v Gotts* [1980] 1 WLR 521.

On the other hand, a mere increase in the number of the caravans using the dominant tenement, which would thus result in a more intensive use of the right of way, was held not to constitute excessive user of the way in question, in *British Railways Board v Glass* [1965] Ch 538. As Davies LJ said in this case (at p 568): 'If there is a right of way to and from a particular house, it does not seem that the owner of the servient tenement could successfully complain if the number of persons living in the house was greatly increased, or if the occupier of the house chose to use the right of way very much more frequently than formerly.' A mere increase in the number of persons using the way will not normally amount to an excessive user (*Woodhouse & Co Ltd v Kirkland Ltd* [1970] 1 WLR 1185). But the building of a new house on the dominant tenement would normally amount to excessive user (*Bracewell v Appleby* [1975] Ch 408).

4 Acquisition of rights: prescription

A private right of way may arise by either of the two principal methods in which public rights of way arise, ie by grant or by implication, but of course the provisions of the Highways Act 1980, s 31 do not apply here. In addition, a private right of way may arise by prescription or presumed grant under the Prescription Act 1832, s 2 of which provides as follows:

In claims of rights of way or other easements the periods to be twenty years and forty years—No claim which may be lawfully made at the common law, by custom, prescription, or grant, to any way or other easement, or to any watercourse, or the use of any water, to be enjoyed or derived upon, over, or from any land or water of our said lord the King . . . or being parcel of . . . the duchy of Cornwall, or being the property of any ecclesiastical or lay person, or body corporate, when such way or other matter as herein last before mentioned shall have been actually enjoyed by any person claiming right thereto without interruption for the full period of twenty years, shall be defeated or destroyed by showing only that such way or other matter was first enjoyed at any time prior to such period of twenty years, but nevertheless such claim may be defeated in any other way by which the same is now liable to be defeated; and where such way or other matter as herein last before mentioned shall have been so enjoyed as afore-said for the full period of forty years, the right thereto shall be deemed absolute and indefeasible, unless it shall appear that the same was enjoyed by some comment or agreement expressly given or made for that purpose by deed or writing.

This should be contrasted with s 31(1) of the Act of 1980, (see p 35). The comments on that section apply generally also to private rights of way—in fact, the principles of the 1832 Act were adopted and adapted as the basis of the 1932 statute, which was the predecessor of s 31, though the Prescription Act applies only to private rights. However, it is not sufficient, in claiming under the Prescription Act 1832 (as it is under s 31), to be able to establish that the way in question has been enjoyed *nec vi, nec clam, nec precario*, for a period of 20 years, as in addition it must be established that the period is one next before the commencement of some suit or action wherein the claim to which the period relates is brought in question: *Reilly v Orange* [1955] 2 QB 112.

Where a right is given by permission the user must remain permissive and it is 'not capable of ripening into a right, save where the permission is oral and the user has continued for forty or sixty years [under the 1832 Act; the 60 years refers to profits à prendre], unless and until, having been given for a limited period only, it expires, or being general it is revoked or there is a change in circumstances from which revocation may fairly be implied' (*per* Goff J in *Healey v Hawkins* [1968] 3 All ER 836, at p 841). See also *Green v Ashco Horticulturist Ltd* [1966] 1 WLR 889. In *Jones v Price and Morgan* (1992) 64 P & CR 404, the Court of Appeal held that a user which continues on a common understanding, between the landowner and claimant, that the user is permissive, negatives the existence of a claim of right under the Prescription Act 1832, s 2.

Further, by the Prescription Act 1832, s 4 no act or other matter is to be deemed to be an interruption, such as will prevent the period from running, unless it has been submitted to or acquiesced in for at least one year; as to this point, see *Davies v Du Paver* [1953] 1 QB 184 and *Goldsmith v Burrow Construction Co Ltd* (1987) *The Times*, 31 July. The owner of the servient tenement must have been aware, either personally or through his agents, of the user of the way by the owner of the dominant tenement: *Diment v NH Foot Ltd* [1974] 1 WLR 1427 and *Ironside, Crabb and Crabb v Cook, Cook and Barefoot* (1980), 41 P & CR 326.

A private right of way enforceable against a fee simple owner cannot arise by agreement between tenant and tenant, nor by one tenant as against another tenant. It can only be acquired by the owner of the dominant tenement against the owner of the servient tenement, in conformity with 'the essential notion of a right by prescription, namely, that the right is acquired by the owner of land over land belonging to another owner' (*per* Collins MR in *Kilgour v Gaddes* [1904] 1 KB, at p 460 as applied in *Simmons v Dobson* [1991] 4 All ER 25). However, although an easement cannot be acquired by prescription as against a tenant of the servient property, the period will commence to run provided the owner was in possession at the commencement of the period; the twenty years will not cease because there is later a tenant. Moreover, a tenant can prescribe on behalf of his landlord. On these points, see *Pugh v Savage* [1970] QB 373. The period of prescription will not necessarily be broken by a change in the precise route of the way, if this has been arranged by agreement between the parties: *Davis v Whitby* [1974] Ch 186.

But the owner of the right is not necessarily the only person who may exercise it. Other persons may avail themselves of this right if their particular circumstances are duly considered. If, for example, the right has arisen by express grant, then the instrument by which it has been created will be sufficient indication if due attention is paid to the nature of the land itself and the several purposes of the grant. This means, for example, in the ordinary case of a grant of a right of way to a private dwelling house, that not only the grantee but also members of his family, servants, visitors, guests and tradespeople, though none of these persons be expressly mentioned in the grant, may use the way (see *per* Swinfen Eady J in *Basendale v North Lambeth etc Club* [1902] 2 Ch 426, at p 429, in which the grant referred to 'the lessee his executors, administrators and assigns, undertenants and servants', giving them the right of passage.

A claim to a right of way may also be based on long user, apart from the Act of 1832. At common law, this meant immemorial user, dating back to 1189; in practice, very long user would be accepted, provided no evidence was available to show that at some time in the past, the way could not have existed (eg because the *locus in quo* was once covered by the sea, which subsequently receded).

Prescription is really based on a presumed lost grant, and user may be based on the fiction of a 'lost modern grant', under which 20 years' user at *any* time may be sufficient: *RCP Holdings v Rogers* [1953] 1 All ER 1029. Furthermore, a claim based upon the lost modern grant concept may still be valid even where the user has acted on a misunderstanding as to the nature of his rights: *Bridle v Ruby* [1988] 3 All ER 64. The doctrine of acquisition by prescription (by any of the three methods) cannot be used to acquire any right less than a right in fee simple: *Wheaton v Maple & Co* [1893] Ch 48. Nor can prescription be used to acquire a right that is prohibited by statute (*Hanning v Top Deck Travel Group Ltd* (1993) *The Times*, 6 May (right to drive vehicles across Horsell Common prohibited by s 193 of the Law of Property Act 1925)). If a claim is made to a right of way over a churchyard, it seems it will succeed if the facts are consistent with the grant of such a right by a faculty which has since been lost: see the county court case of *Macnally* v *Digby* [1957] JPL 583, where the facts were not sufficient to establish such a right.

5 Acquisition of rights: express grant or reservation

The nature and extent of a private right of way existing by virtue of an express grant or by reservation should be clear from a construction of the instrument by which it was created. In the event of questions arising as to the interpretation of such an instrument, not only its language but the circumstances under which it was executed, the nature of and description of both dominant and servient tenements and all other material considerations will be reviewed. In *White* v *Richards* (1993) *The Times*, 22 March, the Court of Appeal endorsed the interpretation of the words 'the track' in a conveyance by means of evidence regarding the physical characteristics of the route at the time of the reservation. The Court also upheld an injunction specifying the maximum width and weight of vehicles entitled to use the right of way.

If the dominant tenement is not clearly described in the document creating the easement, the court is apparently entitled to have regard to the surrounding circumstances in order to identify it: *Johnstone* v *Holdway* [1963] QB 601; and *The Shannon Ltd* v *Venner Ltd* [1965] Ch 682. In case of doubt the court will lean in favour of the grantee as against the grantor, following the general rule of law (see *Ballard* v *Dyson*, p 109) that a strict interpretation is to be placed upon the limitations of a grant, and this rule is to be applied also to reservations in a conveyance in favour of the grantee, so that although such a reservation amounts to a grant to the vendor by the purchaser, it is to be construed against the purchaser. But this presumption is to be applied in the light of the surrounding circumstances, and only when the words of the grant (or reservation) are wholly ambiguous (*St Edmundsbury and Ipswich Board of Finance* v *Clark* (*No 2*) [1975] 1 WLR 468). In particular, it would not be inferred, from the fact that the field across which a prescriptive right of way ran was agricultural, that the way could be used for the purposes of a camping ground: *RCP Holdings Ltd* v *Rogers* [1953] 1 All ER 1029. There are, however, certain implied interpretations which the courts have recognised as being reasonable.

Thus, in *Cannon v Villars* (1878) 8 Ch D 415, where a tenant had a means of ingress and egress through an entrance under the landlord's house to business premises, it was held that the tenant had an implied right of way for horses and carts as well as foot passengers, and could get an injunction against the landlord for obstructing the gateway. In *Newcomen v Coulson* (1877) 5 Ch D 133, it was held that when a right of way is granted to 'the owner and owners for the time being' of lands, and the lands are subsequently severed, the grant gives a right of way to the owner for the time being of every part of the severed lands. See also, generally, *White v Grand Hotel Eastbourne Ltd* [1913] 1 Ch 113, applied in *Todrick v Western National Omnibus Co Ltd* [1934] Ch 561; and *Robinson v Bailey* [1948] 2 All ER 791.

6 Acquisition of rights: implied grant

There are certain implications of law which automatically create rights of way. Where dominant and servient tenements have previously been in the same ownership and the owner has disposed of a portion, the law implies in favour of the dominant tenement such rights of way as had previously been enjoyed by the owner over his own land and are reasonably necessary for its use and occupation—provided, that is, that no contrary intention is expressed in the conveyance (see *Wheeldon v Burrows* (1879) 12 Ch D 31).

Sometimes it will happen that a right of way has been granted to a particular place or building for its necessary enjoyment, but the use of the place or building may have been changed entirely. Thus, in *Henning v Burnet* (1852) 8 Ex 187 where, on the sale of certain premises and a field with all ways usually held, occupied or enjoyed therewith, with free liberty of ingress, egress and regress for the purchaser's cattle and carriages over the carriage road leading to the premises, the purchaser made a gate from the field abutting onto the carriage road into the road at an intermediate part thereof and drove horses and carriages along the road into the field and back again, it was held that the purchaser was trespassing, the right of way being to the premises only. In *White v Grand Hotel Eastbourne Ltd* [1913] 1 Ch 113, it was held that, where there was a verbal agreement by one party to set back a party wall in order to give more convenient access and by the other to grant a right of way to a gate 9 ft wide to be made in the wall, on the widening of the gate to 15 ft there was no right of way except to a gate of the original size and in the original place.

In *South Eastern Railway Co v Cooper* [1924] 1 Ch 211, a railway company when constructing the line granted a level crossing to the owners of certain lands in order that they might have access to a highway with a roadway for carts, etc. The way had originally been used only for agricultural traffic, but a short time before the action a sand pit had been opened and the traffic over the crossing greatly increased and became of a commercial character. The company brought an action for a declaration of the crossing as an accommodation work and an injunction to restrict the traffic to agricultural traffic. It was held that this was not the case, and the declaration and injunction were refused.

There is also what is known as a 'way of necessity' (on this subject, see 24 Convy (NS) 205)—a right of way implied over another man's land where the claimant has no other means of access to his own land. This way of necessity is based upon an implied grant, either by a grantor or by statute, but it is not available to a 'squatter' who secures title by 12 years' undisturbed possession under the Limitation Act 1980 (see *Wilkes v Greenway* (1890) 6 TLR 449; *Corporation of London v Riggs* (1880) 13 Ch D 798; *Union Lighterage Co v London Graving Dock Co* [1902] 2 Ch 557, 573; *Pearson v Spencer* (1861) 1 B & S 571). It applies whether the close for which the way is claimed is totally enclosed by the grantor's land, or partly by his land and partly by land owned by other persons whom the owner of the close cannot compel to give him any legal right of way (see *Barry v Hasseldine* [1952] Ch 835). Ways of necessity are limited by the necessity existing at the time of the grant and cannot be used for other purposes: see *Corporation of London v Riggs* (above).

A way of necessity may be implied (in the absence of express grant) over a common staircase leading to flats in a block: *Devine v London Housing Society Ltd* [1950] 2 All ER 1173. But note the unwillingness of the Court of Appeal to find an implied way of necessity through the use of public policy in *Nickerson v Barraclough* [1981] Ch 426.

A right of way may be implied where the circumstances under which the grant was made so necessitate: *Pwllbach Colliery Company Ltd v Woodman* [1915] AC 634. In *Stafford v Lee* (1993) 65 P & CR 172, the Court of Appeal held that where the grantee can establish a common intention, between grantor and grantee, that the subject of the grant shall be used in a particular manner, the law will imply the grant of such easements as may be necessary to give effect to it.

So, the Court determined that a grant of land in 1955 was subject to a common intention that it would be used for the construction of a residential dwelling and that it was, therefore, necessary to imply a right of way to and from that land for the purposes of constructing and using the dwelling.

7 Acquisition of rights: implied reservation

This is rare and will be implied in favour of a grantor only in cases of necessity or where such a reservation was clearly intended by the parties (see, eg *Re Webb's Lease* [1951] Ch 808).

8 Acquisition of rights: by statute

The Law of Property Act 1925, s 62 provides, *inter alia*, as follows:

(1) A conveyance of land shall be deemed to include and shall by virtue of this Act operate to convey, with the land, all buildings, erections, fixtures, commons, hedges, ditches, fenches, ways, waters, watercourses, liberties, privileges, easements, rights, and advantages whatsoever, appertaining or reputed to appertain to the land, or any part thereof, or, at the time of conveyance, demised, occupied, or enjoyed with or reputed or known as part or parcel of or appurtenant to the land or any part thereof.

(2) A conveyance of land, having houses or other buildings thereon, shall be deemed to include and shall by virtue of this Act operate to convey, with the land, houses, or other buildings, all outhouses, erections, fixtures, cellars, areas, courts, courtyards, cisterns, sewers, gutters, drains, ways, passages, lights, watercourses, liberties, privileges, easements, rights, and advantages whatsoever, appertaining or reputed to appertain to the land, houses, or other buildings conveyed, or any of them, or any part thereof, of, at the time of conveyance, demised, occupied, or enjoyed with, or reputed or known as part or parcel of or appurtenant to, the land, houses, or other buildings, conveyed, or any of them, or any part thereof.

(3) [Relates to manors and manorial incidents.]

(4) This section applies only if and as far as a contrary intention is not expressed in the conveyance, and has effect subject to the terms of the conveyance and to the provisions therein contained.

(5) This section shall not be construed as giving to any person a better title to any property, right, or thing in this section mentioned than the title which the conveyance gives to him to the land or manor expressed to be conveyed, or as conveying to him any property, right,

or thing in this section mentioned, further or otherwise than as the same could have been involved to him by the conveying parties.

(6) This section applies to conveyances made after the thirty-first day of December, eighteen hundred and eighty-one.

This section has the same effect as a pre-1882 conveyance including the 'general words' used by conveyancers; for recent cases in which the section has been applied, see *Wright v Macadam* [1949] 2 KB 744; *Goldberg v Edwards* [1950] Ch 247; and *Ward v Kirkland* [1967] Ch 194 and *Graham v Philcox* [1984] QB 747.

With regard to this, see *International Tea Stores Co v Hobbs* [1903] 2 Ch 165, where it was laid down that, in order to show that the use of a way is 'enjoyed with' the land within the similar terms (now repealed) of the Conveyancing Act 1881, s 6 and that a right to such use passes on a conveyance of the land by virtue of that section, it is *prima facie* sufficient, in the absence of rebutting circumstances, to prove that the use was *de facto* enjoyed at the time of conveyance. 'Conveyance' in s 62 includes a lease, but not a contract or an agreement for a lease, as these create only equitable rights: *Borman v Griffith* [1930] 1 Ch 493.

In addition, a local authority may acquire a right of way without the agreement of the servient owner, by including in a compulsory purchase order the acquisition of such a 'new right'. The order has to be made in the normal manner and authorised by a Minister of the Crown (Local Government (Miscellaneous Provisions) Act 1976, s 13, as amended by the Acquisition of Land Act 1981, Sched 4, para 26).

9 'Jus spatiandi'

It seems that a *jus spatiandi*, a right to wander at will over a defined area of land (the servient tenement), is capable of being acquired as an easement, if it is attached to and capable of benefiting a dominant tenement (*Re Ellenborough Park* [1956] Ch 131 at p 153), although such a right to wander at will cannot be acquired as a public right of way, as the public right must have a terminus *a quo* and a terminus *ad quem* (*Att-Gen v Antrobus* [1905] 2 Ch 188). There may now be public rights of access, eg to Stonehenge, which was in issue in the *Antrobus* case, and is now secured, subject to local regulations under the Ancient Monuments and Archaeological Areas Act 1979, and the National Heritage Act 1983 (see p 106); but note the recent controversies over access to the stones during the time of the summer solstice.

10 Maintenance and repair

In the absence of agreement to the contrary, when a private right of way is granted, the grantor is under no obligation either to construct a roadway: *Newcomen v Coulson* (1877) 5 Ch D 133, 143 or to maintain it in repair for the benefit of the grantee: *Jones v Pritchard* [1908] 1 Ch 630, 638). But the grantee is entitled to enter upon the land of the grantor for the purpose of constructing a roadway adequate for the purpose of the grant made to him, and this right extends to entering for the purpose of doing repairs and restoration where necessary from time to time: *Newcomen v Coulson; Jones v Pritchard*, and *Rudd v Rea* [1921] 1 Ir R 223). An agreement by which the grant is subject to repair by the grantee is a conditional easement, and therefore may be binding upon all successors of the original grantee (*Duncan v Louch* (1845) 6 QB 904).

Moreover, in *Holden v White* [1982] QB 679, the Court of Appeal held that the owner of servient land was only liable under the Occupiers' Liability Act 1957, to her visitors and not to other persons who might be lawfully using the right of way. Hence, the landowner was not liable for the injuries suffered by a milkman using the right of way who fell through a broken manhole cover which formed part of the pathway (note: this decision has been subject to academic criticism (see 98 LQR 541)).

Where a person has obtained a prescriptive right of way, he is not entitled to make improvements to the path or road which would benefit his own land to the detriment of the owner of the land over which the right of way is exercised. Hence, the replacement of a rough track with a stone road amounted to improvement, going far beyond mere repair, and was a trespass: (*Mills v Silver* [1991] 1 All ER 449).

11 Obstruction and disturbance

Interference of any sort with the rights of a grantee is an actionable nuisance if it is a disturbance of those rights of an unreasonable nature, keeping in mind the fact that a grant of passage does not give any exclusive right of user to the grantee. See, generally, *Thorpe v Brumfitt* (1873) LR 8 Ch 650; *Clifford v Hoare* (1874) LR 9 CP 362; *Lane v Capsey* [1891] 3 Ch 411; *Weston v Laurence Weaver Ltd* [1961] 1 QB 402, *Saint v Jenner* [1973] Ch 275 and *Celsteel Ltd v Alton House Holdings Ltd* [1986] 1 WLR 512. A grantee aggrieved may bring proceedings in the county court for damages and seek an injunction against the grantor to prevent obstruction of the right of way. A grantor's failure to clear the route of frozen snow and ice does not amount to an actionable obstruction: *Cluttenham v Anglian Water Authority* (1986) *The Times*, 14 August.

12 Extinguishment

A private right of way may be extinguished like any other easement by statute, destruction, express release (which must be by deed: *Lovell v Smith* (1857) 3 CB (NS) 120), or even by implied release (ibid). In the latter case, the implication must rest upon the intention of the owner of the dominant tenement which will be presumed from his conduct (*Crossley & Sons Ltd v Lightowler* (1867) LR 2 Ch 478). Mere non-user of the grant is not of itself sufficient to justify implied release, though it may be an element to be considered (*James v Stevenson* [1893] AC 162 and *Williams v Usherwood* (1983) 45 P & CR 235). In *Benn v Hardinge* (1992) *The Times*, 13 October, the Court of Appeal held that because a private right of way was a valuable property right it should not lightly be inferred that it had been abandoned. There a right of way had not been used for 175 years, as the owner of the dominant land had another access to the fields concerned, and the Court refused to find an intention to abandon the right through such non-user. Extinguishment of a public right of way by statutory process does not of itself extinguish a private right over the same way: (*Walsh v Oates* [1953] 1 QB 578; *Shonleigh Nominees v Att-Gen* [1974] 1 WLR 305).

Provision is made in several statutes for the extinguishment of private rights of way over land purchased or appropriated by a public body in the exercise of statutory powers (see the Housing Act 1985, s 295, the Town and Country Planning Act 1990, s 236 and the New Towns Act 1981, s 19 for examples). Where land over which a private right of way runs is compulsorily acquired, and the right of way is extinguished under one or other of these statutory powers, the person entitled to the right will be entitled to compensation from the acquiring authority, to be assessed in accordance with the general principles of the Land Compensation Act 1961 subject to any special provisions in the enabling statute.

13 The Access to Neighbouring Land Act 1992

Where a person does not benefit from a private right of way over neighbouring land, but requires access to such land in order to undertake repair work on his own property, the person must seek the permission of his neighbour or risk an action in trespass. However, personal animosity between neighbours may prevent such permission being granted or an unreasonable licence fee may be demanded. Hence in 1985 the Law Commission (in Report No 151) recommended the creation of a statutory right of access for neighbours to undertake necessary repair work. A modified version of that right has been enacted as the Access to Neighbouring Land Act 1992. Section 1 entitles a person (who may be an estate owner, tenant or licensee) to apply to the court—initially the county court for the district in which the dominant land is situated (s 7(2) and SI 1992 No 3348) for an access order permitting entry to adjoining or adjacent land (the servient land). The court may make an order for work that is 'reasonably necessary for the preservation of the whole or any part of the dominant land' (s 1(2)(a)); this phrase includes the following types of work:

(1) the maintenance, repair or renewal of any part of a building or other structure comprised in, or situate on, the dominant land;

(2) the clearance, repair or renewal of any drain, sewer, pipe or cable so comprised or situate;

(3) the treatment, cutting back, felling, removal or replacement of any hedge, tree, shrub or other growing thing which is so comprised and which is, or is in danger of becoming, damaged, diseased, dangerous, insecurely rooted or dead; and

(4) the filling in, or clearance, of any ditch so comprised (s 1(4)).

Provided that the work cannot be carried out or would be substantially more difficult to carry out, without entry upon the servient land (s 1(2)(b)); the court cannot make an order where the effect would be to cause the occupier of the servient land to suffer unreasonable hardship or interference with his enjoyment of the land (s 1(3)). Where an access order is made it must specify:

(1) the work to the dominant land that may be carried out;

(2) the particular area of the servient land that may be entered; and

(3) the date, or period during which, the servient land may be entered (s 2(1)).

Conditions may be imposed on the access order which the court considers to be reasonably necessary for avoiding or restricting,

(1) loss, damage or injury to persons occupying the servient land and

(2) loss of privacy by such persons (s 2(2)).

Other conditions may require the applicant to be insured against risks created by the authorised work and to pay compensation to the respondent for damage caused to the servient land (s 2(4)). Where the dominant land is not 'residential land' (defined in s 2(7) as land consisting of a dwelling, the curtilage of a dwelling and parts of buildings used mainly with dwellings), the court may order the applicant to pay the respondent a 'fair and reasonable' sum of money for the privilege of being able to enter the servient land (s 2(5)). An access order cannot authorise an applicant to leave anything (eg pipes or supports) permanently in, on or over the servient land (s 3(2)). Section 4(4) makes void any agreement, whenever made, which purports to prevent a person from applying for an access order. Where a court grants an access order it is binding upon the respondent and any of his successors in title to the servient land, provided that it has been properly registered by the applicant (for unregistered land as a writ or order under s 6(1) of the Land Charges Act 1972, using Form K4; and for registered land by notice under s 49 of the Land Registration Act 1925) (ss 4(1) and 5).

When an access order has been made, the applicant or any person bound by the order may apply to the court for a discharge, variation or suspension of any terms or conditions in the order (s 6(1)). If a person fails to comply with the terms of an access order, which are binding upon him, the court may order him to pay damages to an applicant who has been adversely affected by the failure (s 6(2)); this sanction is without prejudice to any other remedies available to the court (eg an injunction). The Act came into force on 31 January 1993 (SI 1992 No 3349).

The County Court Rules Order 49, r 1 details the procedure for seeking an access order (SI 1992 No 3348). The application must be made by an originating application filed with the county court for the district in which the dominant land is situated (r 1(2)). The respondent shall be the owner and occupier of the servient land, and if he wishes to be heard on the application he must file an answer within 14 days after the date of service of the application on him (rule 1(4)). The application must contain the following information:

(1) the identity of the dominant and the servient land, and whether the former is or includes residential land;

(2) details of the works alleged to be necessary for the preservation of the dominant land;

(3) why entry upon the servient land is required and details of the area to which access is required (where possible this should be marked on a plan annexed to the application);

(4) the name of the person who will be undertaking the works (if known at the time of the application);

(5) the proposed date on which, or the dates between which, the works are to be started and their approximate duration; and

(6) what, if any, provision has been made by way of insurance in the event of possible injury to persons or damage to property arising out of the proposed works (r 1(3)).

The application may be heard and determined by the district judge and the court can deal with it in chambers (if the court thinks fit) (rule 1(7)). Further guidance on such applications can be found in *The County Court Practice 1993* at pp 525–535.

Whilst the above Act provides a useful remedy of last resort, lawyers have been cautioned against encouraging clients to invoke this procedure as it may lead to lengthy and costly proceedings. Only if negotiations have failed to achieve an agreement on access should an application under the Act be contemplated.

Model Adoption Agreement under Section 38 Highways Act 1980

This agreement is made the _____ day of _____
between _____ whose registered office is
at _____ (the Company) (1) _____ whose registered
office is at _____ (the Surety) (2) and the _____
Council of _____ ('the Council') (3)

WHEREAS

(1) The Company is the freeholder of the land shown on the
attached plan and is capable of dedicating as a public highway
the land shown coloured brown (hereinafter called 'the street') on
the said plan.

(2) The Council is willing to do all acts necessary for the taking
over and adoption of the street as a highway maintainable at the
public expense in accordance with the Agreement.

(3) The Surety has agreed to enter into this Agreement for the
purpose of securing the due performance of the terms conditions
provisions and stipulations herein contained on the part of the
Company (or in default by the Council).

NOW in pursuance of section 38 of the Highways Act 1980 section
33 of the Local Government (Miscellaneous Provisions) Act 1982
section 106 of the Town and Country Planning Act 1990 and of all
other enabling powers IT IS AGREED as follows:

1 The company hereby declares and warrants to the Council that
   it has full right liberty or consent to carry out such works as
   may be necessary to join the street to an existing public highway.

2   The Company covenants with the Council

(a) That it will properly construct sewer level pave metal flag channel kerb drain light and otherwise make good the street (hereinafter referred to as 'the works') in all respects to the satisfaction of the Council's Engineer (hereinafter referred to as 'the Engineer') and in the position shown on the plan annexed hereto and shall in the course of the works cause and permit all necessary gas and water mains and electricity cables and other services including sewers and drains for any building erected on the land to be laid under or in the street.

(b) That it will before commencing the works give to the Engineer at least seven days notice in writing of its intention to commence (or when the construction of the works has in the opinion of the Engineer whose opinion shall be the final ceased for more than four weeks to recommence) and when giving such notice the Company will submit to the Engineer for inspection any contract drawings or other documents relating thereto.

(c) That it will proceed with the works with all due diligence and will complete the same to the satisfaction of the Engineer within twelve months from the date hereof provided that:

(i) the said twelve month period may be extended for such period or periods as the Council may in its absolute discretion determine (whether or not an application for such extension has been made by the Company) and on the same terms as contained herein or on such additional or amended terms as may be agreed between the parties hereto

(ii) at the end of the said twelve month period or any extension thereof the Council shall have in its absolute discretion the right firstly to enter onto the land to construct or complete the works and secondly to recover the expenses of such construction or completion from the Company or in the Council's discretion from the Surety which said expenses shall be payable on demand.

(d) That it will before carrying out the work of connecting the street with the carriageway of any existing adopted highway or highways give notice to such person or persons board or authority being the statutory undertakers for the time being of any service or services laid in upon or under such existing highway or highways of the proposal to make such connection as if the connection were a work to be executed for road purposes and were mentioned in The New Roads and Street Works Act 1991 and shall indemnify the Council from the cost of any works or measures deemed necessary by the statutory undertakers in consequence of the proposal to make such connection.

(e) That it will during the progress of the works give to the Engineer and any person or persons duly authorised by him free access to every part of the street and the land and permit him or them to inspect the street and all materials used or intended to be used therein and shall give effect to any requirement made or instruction given by the Engineer or any person or persons duly authorised by him.

(f) That it will until the street shall become as hereinafter provided a highway maintainable at the public expense keep the whole of the works in a good state of efficiency and repair and will reinstate and make good any defects which shall or may appear arise or become manifest to the Engineer and the Engineer may until the street shall become a highway maintainable at the public expense require the Company to make good any portion of the works which he reasonably considers to be defective and require the reconstruction of the same by the Company and in default thereof the Council shall after one month's notice (or any lesser period specified by the Engineer where he considers that the defect should be remedied as a matter of urgency) in writing to the Company of its intention to do so have the right firstly to enter onto the land to make good the works and secondly charge the expenses thereof against the Company (or the Surety if appropriate) which said expenses shall be payable on demand.

(g) That it will not at any time permit the erection and maintenance in on or over the street of any kiosks poles overhead wires or similar structures without the previous consent in writing of the Engineer.

(h) That it will upon receipt of a certificate of substantial completion from the Engineer fully maintain the works for a period of twelve months therefrom or such extension thereof as may be granted or required by the Engineer (hereinafter referred to as 'the maintenance period') and at its own expense maintain repair reinstate and make good or cause to be so maintained repaired reinstated and made good to the satisfaction of the Engineer all defects arising during the maintenance period in any of the works to be executed by the Company under this Deed and carry out all necessary street sweeping and gully cleansing on the streets.

(i) That it will not assign this deed or the benefit or burden thereof nor without the previous consent in writing of the Engineer make any sub-contract for the construction completion·or maintenance of the works hereinbefore specified or any parts or parts thereof.

(j) That it will indemnify and keep indemnified the Council from and against all claims for damages charges compensation or otherwise arising directly or indirectly from the carrying out of the works and against all costs and expenses incurred in connection therewith.

(k) That it will pay to the Council upon completion of this Deed:
   (i) all legal costs and charges reasonably incurred by the Council incidental to the preparation and completion of this Agreement and duplicate thereof and
   (ii) the administrative and supervision charges of the Engineer in the sum of £ _____ .

(l) That in the event of the Council exercising default powers under this Agreement then the Company will allow the Council full and free access to the land for all purposes connected with the exercise of these powers.

(m) That it will not commence or cause to be or allow to be commenced the erection of a building on any part of the land until the street has been excavated sewered (including connection to the appropriate main sewer) levelled and the hard core foundation laid complete in all respects to the satisfaction of the Engineer.

(n) That it will not permit any of the buildings fronting the street to be occupied until the street has been constructed to base course level to the satisfaction of the Engineer and the street lighting has been installed and is operational to the satisfaction of the Engineer.

(o) The Company shall immediately upon the execution of this Agreement dedicate the street as a highway for use by the public.

3 The Council covenants with the Company as

(a) At the end of the maintenance period and when the Engineer is satisfied that the Company has duly and properly carried out all cleansing works and also repaired and made good all defects arising during that time the Engineer shall issue a certificate of final completion PROVIDED THAT such certificate shall not be issued until all pipes wires cables conduits and other apparatus necessary for carrying oil gas water electricity telephone connections and foul and surface water sewage have been laid within the street or otherwise in accordance with the specifications and plans annexed hereto or submitted to the Engineer under Clause 2(d) hereof and connected respectively to all the dwellinghouses erected on the land and to suitable mains outfalls or other associated drainage works.

(b) That it will upon the issue of the certificate of final completion referred to in Clause 3(a) hereof cause the street to become a highway maintainable at the public expense and thereafter the same shall accordingly become and be such a highway.

4 The Surety hereby covenants with the Council that if the Company at any time fails to perform or observe any of the covenants on its part contained in this Deed or if the Company shall have a Receiving Order in bankruptcy made against it or go into liquidation voluntarily or otherwise or shall execute a Deed of Assignment for the benefit of creditors (except for the purpose of amalgamation or reconstruction) but without prejudice to the right of the Council to exercise all or any of its rights and powers under the Highways Act 1980 or any other statutory provision of any other right claim or remedy against the Company for such non-performance or non-observance THE SURETY shall within twenty eight days pay to the Council such sum of money as may be estimated by the Engineer to be required to complete or properly execute the works and to maintain the same and make good all defects for a period of twelve months prior to the adoption of the street as a highway maintainable at the public expense together with such amount as will cover the Council's usual establishment charges PROVIDED ALWAYS that the sum payable by the Surety shall not in any event exceed the sum stipulated in the Schedule.

5   It is hereby agreed and declared by and between the parties hereto as follows:

(a) Nothing herein contained shall operate to take away or prejudice the right of the Council to exercise the statutory powers conferred upon it if the Company or the Surety shall fail to perform all or any of the obligations undertaken by or imposed upon the Company and the Surety by the Deed in the manner hereinbefore provided nor imply any obligation on the part of the Council to the Company or the Surety or any person or persons to ensure that the works are properly constructed.

(b) If the Company shall fail to perform or observe any of the conditions on the part of the Company contained herein or if the Company shall have a Receiving Order in bankruptcy made against him or go into liquidation voluntarily or otherwise or shall execute a Deed of Assignment for the benefit of creditors (except for the purpose of amalgamation or reconstruction) the Council may without prejudice to any of their rights claims or remedies against the Company or Surety for such non-performance or non-observance determine this Deed by notice in writing signed by the Council's Solicitor and delivered to the Company or sent by post to the address stated in this Deed.

IN WITNESS whereof the parties hereto have caused their respective Common Seals to be hereunto affixed to this Deed the day and year first before written.

Schedule

The liability of the Surety under this Agreement shall not exceed £ _____ .

High Court Statement of Claim and Defence— Breach of Section 41 Highways Act 1980 and/or Negligence

In the High Court of Justice   19_____ B _____
Maintown District Registry
Writ Issued the _____ day of _____ 19____

BETWEEN:

ARTHUR BROWN   Plaintiff
and
BLANKSHIRE COUNTY COUNCIL   Defendant

STATEMENT OF CLAIM

1 The Defendant is and was at all material times the highway authority responsible for the maintenance of the highway known as High Street Maintown in the county of Blankshire.

2 On or about the 1st day of August 1993 the Plaintiff was walking along the pavement of High Street when he tripped against a cavity adjoining a broken paving slab which was some 2 inches deep, and he fell and thereby suffered injury.

3 The Plaintiff's accident was caused by the Defendant's breach of its statutory duty under section 41 of the Highways Act 1980 and/or the negligence of the Defendant its servants or agents.

Particulars of breach of statutory duty and/or negligence

(i) Failing in time adequately or at all to repair and/or maintain the said pavement.

(ii) Failing to devise, institute and operate any or any adequate system for inspecting the said pavement.

(iii) Failing to heed and/or act upon the results of such inspections as were made (none being admitted) which ought to have revealed the presence of the said cavity and the consequent dangerous state of the pavement.

(iv) Failing, prior to the Plaintiff's accident rather than afterwards as in fact occurred to fill, level or otherwise render harmless the said cavity.

(v) Failing, whether by the provision of warning signs, barriers or otherwise, to highlight the presence of the said cavity in the pavement and/or to divert pedestrians around or away therefrom.

(vi) In the premises, exposing the Plaintiff to a foreseeable and unnecessary risk of injury.

4   Further or alternatively the said pavement in the aforesaid defective and dangerous condition constituted a nuisance which was caused, continued or adopted by the Defendant its servants or agents.

5   By reason of the matters complained of, the Plaintiff has suffered pain, injury, loss and damages.

Particulars of Injury

[*Set out a brief outline of the injuries and refer to a Consultant's medical report which is required to be served with the Statement of Claim*]

Particulars of Special Damage

A full Schedule of Special Damages is served with the Statement of Claim.

6   The Plaintiff is entitled to and claims interest upon all sums awarded, pursuant to section 35A of the Supreme Court Act 1981 at such rate and for such period as the Court deems just.

AND the Plaintiff claims:

(i) Damages
(ii) Interest thereon as aforesaid pursuant to section 35A of the Supreme Court Act 1981.

Served etc.

In the High Court of Justice   19____ B ____
Maintown District Registry
Writ Issued the _____ day of _____ 19____

BETWEEN:

ARTHUR BROWN   Plaintiff
and
BLANKSHIRE COUNTY COUNCIL   Defendant

DEFENCE

---

1 Paragraph 1 of the Statement of Claim is admitted.

2 Save that it is admitted that the Plaintiff has suffered an accident paragraph 2 of the Statement of Claim is not admitted and the Plaintiff is put to strict proof of the circumstances of the alleged accident.

3 Paragraph 3 of the Statement of Claim is denied and each and every alleged Particular of breach of statutory duty and/or negligence is denied as if each were set out here and denied.

4 Paragraph 4 of the Statement of Claim is denied.

5 It is the Defendant's case that High Street was safe for the reasonably careful pedestrian.

6 The Defendant will rely upon the statutory defence afforded by section 58 of the Highways Act 1980.

7 Further or in the alternative, if, which is denied, the Plaintiff proves that his accident occurred as alleged or at all the Defendant will contend that it was caused or materially contributed to by the Plaintiff's own negligence.

Particulars of Contributory Negligence

    (i) Failing to look where he was going;
    (ii) Failing to appreciate the alleged cavity in the footway;
    (iii) Failing to look where he was putting his feet;
    (iv) Failing to walk around or otherwise avoid the alleged cavity;
    (v) Having tripped, failing to regain his balance;
    (vi) In the premises failing to have any or any sufficient regard for his own safety.

8 No admissions are made as to any injury, loss, damage or entitlement to interest whether as alleged in the Statement of Claim or at all. The Plaintiff is put to strict proof of the Particulars of Injury set out in paragraph 5 of the Statement of Claim.

Served etc.

Specimen Information and Summons Alleging an Offence under Section 137 Highways Act 1980

In the County of Blankshire
Petty Sessional Division of
Maintown

Information and
Summons

Maintown Magistrates' Court

TO THE ACCUSED: Mr Arthur Brown

ADDRESS: 1 High Street
                    Maintown
                    Blankshire

Below are particulars of an Information stating an offence committed by you:

The Alleged Offence

Date: 1 August 1993
Place: Footpath 1 in the parish of Smalltown Maintown Blankshire

Particulars and Statute

Without lawful authority or excuse, the accused did wilfully obstruct the free passage along a highway known as Footpath 1 in the parish of Smalltown by erecting a wire fence across the Footpath, some 100 metres north of its junction with Footpath 2 in the parish of Smalltown contrary to section 137(1) of the Highways Act 1980 as amended.

Informant and
Prosecutor _____

County Solicitor of the Blankshire County Council and duly authorised in this behalf.

Address: County Hall
Maintown
Blankshire

Signed _____

County Solicitor and duly
authorised Officer

Laid on the: _____ day of _____ 19____

The above Information having been laid before me, you are hereby Summoned to appear before the Magistrates' court sitting at the Court House _____ on the _____ day of _____ 19____ to answer to the said Information.

_____
Clerk to the Justices or
Justice of the Peace

Index